D1610524

# Beyond The Far Pavilions

"Of course, there's one thing that no foreigner will ever understand, and that's our enthusiasm for cricket."

# BEYOND THE FAR PAVILIONS

*Compiled by*
Leo Cooper and Allen Synge

PAVILION
MICHAEL JOSEPH

First published in Great Britain in 1986 by
Pavilion Books Limited
196 Shaftesbury Avenue, London WC2H 8JL
in association with Michael Joseph Limited
44 Bedford Square, London WC1B 3DP

*British Library Cataloguing in Publication Data*
Beyond the far pavilions.
   1. Cricket – History
   I. Cooper, Leo      II. Synge, Allen
   796.35'8'09        GV913

   ISBN 1-85145-017-3

Typeset by Rowland Phototypesetting Limited
Bury St Edmunds, Suffolk
Printed and bound by
Billing & Sons Limited, Worcester

**Frontispiece: cartoon by Fougasse,
reproduced by kind permission of *Punch***

# Contents

# Preface

A recent survey of the leisure activities of European executives produced a remarkable statistic: 2.03% of Spanish respondents expressed a preference for cricket. Inevitably the leisure-minded executives of France showed an interest of 0.00%. But there were encouraging digits for Germany – 0.95%, and Italy – 1.27%. Predictably, the leisure active businessmen of Holland and Denmark made a solid start towards double figures – in their preference for our national game, that is to say.

Of course, there are other influences at work. One of us remembers a few early seasons ago watching Clinton of Surrey, in the company of his proud father, complete a century against Sussex at Pat Pocock's verdant Malaga cricket ground. It was difficult to form a complete picture of the scene because we were watching the game on the television set of the Rectory Field clubhouse, Blackheath: but there seemed to be a disappointing absence of genuinely local spectators, apart, that was, from the still snow-clad peaks of the Sierra Nevada and some grazing cows or, more probably, bulls.

And yet somehow a sense of the leisure opportunities cricket provides is percolating through to upwardly mobile Spaniards and indeed their German and Italian counterparts. If our researches into the world's *Far Pavilions* can help to increase the game's international acceptance by so much as 0.01% we will indeed retire happy men.

As it is, we have been heartened by the response 'Far Pavilions One' has produced from correspondents and new friends around the world. Many rich new veins of source material have come to light. For example, who, even ten years ago, could have conceived of a cricket anthology which would contain major contributions from the *Helsinki Cricketer*?

Here, then, is the story of a fish that was killed by a six, of a shark that swallowed the ball, and the Hitler Youth who got completely the wrong end of the stick. But here also, we like to think, is a cumulative impression of a game begun by a collection of top-hatted eccentrics on a windy Hampshire upland spreading in various evolving forms across deserts and through jungles, spanning archipelagoes and slithering over arctic ice to the furthest poles. It is a process which, as we will see, was pioneered by famous stalwarts like Richard Daft and the unquestionably sane W. G. Grace and was carried on by generations of missionaries (famous or merely ardent) in a tradition which reaches right down to David Gower.

The message we get from this anthology is that those far pavilions are far more numerous and far flung than even we thought!

LC & AS, LONDON 1986

# Acknowledgements

Our endeavours would not have been half as successful had it not been for a loyal band of supporters and bag carriers.

First among these is the late Terence Prittie whose loyal service to the noble game and the cause of Anglo-Israeli friendship is well known. Among our team who also produced original material were Malcolm Taylor, Timothy Matthews, Silvester Mazzarella, Yehudit Lipman, Simon Holt, H. H. Robinson, Tony Gill, Jeremy Ward, Tony Sharp and James Shepherd.

The pages of the *Cricketer, Cricketer Annual, Cricketer Spring Annual* and *Wisden Cricket Monthly* proved of invaluable aid; nor could we have produced this anthology without the guidance of *Wisden*. Out of these publications we drew not only the services of David Gower and Henry Blofeld but also those of R. J. Hayter, G. R. Hollingworth, P. S. White, W. J. O'Reilly, A. W. Newsom, Alec Waugh, Irving Rosenwater, Willoughby Turner, E. K. Brown, George Cecil, F. M. R. Stephenson, David Rayvern Allen, J. A. Dean as well as a number of anonymous contributors who included a 'Country Vicar' and a 'Soldier' from the Falklands.

A number of contributors were pressed into service who had first appeared in the pages of the *Helsinki Cricketer, Somme Times, Spectator, Daily Mail, Mail on Sunday* and the *Wall Street Journal*. The team we drew from these pages included Richard Geoffrey Burlingham, Ian Ross, Laurie Pignon, Frederick C. Klein and Norman Down. The fierce correspondence in the pages of the *Times* on the subject was revealed by Marcus Williams in *The Way to Lord's* (Fontana) and was led on to the field of play by Prince K. S. Ranjitsinhji, followed by R. H. Macdonald, Alan C. Jenkins, Harold Lockley, Patrick Howarth, Kenneth L. Harkness and George Watkins. David Watts reported from Japan and even the leader page commented on cricket in Tibet.

We would also like to thank the following publishers who allowed a number of their authors out to bat for us, Rowland Bowen *Cricket: a History of its Growth and Development throughout the World* (Eyre and Spottiswoode), D. W. Saunders and George Smith *Two Cricket Vagrants* (Murray), A. A. Thomson *Odd Men In* (Pavilion Books) and *Cricket my Happiness* (Museum Press), E. W. Swanton *Sort of a Cricket Person* (Collins) and *The World of Cricket* (Michael Joseph), F. S. Ashley-Cooper *Cricket Highways and Byways* (George Allen and Unwin), Bill Frindall in John Sheppard (ed.) *Cricket: More than a Game* (Angus and Robertson), Ralph Stock *Confessions of a Tenderfoot* (Grant Richards), Michael Mackintyre *The New Pacific* (BBC/Collins), Christopher Martin-Jenkins *The Cricket Book of Bizarre Cricketing Records* (Century), Richard Daft *Kings of*

*Cricket* (Arrowsmith), W. G. Grace *'W. G.' Cricketing Reminiscences and Personal Recollections* (J. Bowden), and Richard Gordon *Cricket 72* (Test and County Cricket Board).

We were aided in our activities by a number of members of the Cricket Society: Nigel Haygarth supplied us with news from Japan in the form of Professor Makoto Yamada and the *Kobe Regatta and Athletic Club Magazine*, Christopher Box-Grainger provided us with details of his tours both independently and through the pages of Ted Dexter's and David Lemmon's *A Walk to the Wicket* (George Allen and Unwin), while we have leaned heavily on James D. Coldham's knowledge of cricket in Germany. Further expert information came from the pens of P. C. G. Labouchere, T. A. J. Provis and P. S. Hargreaves in *The Story of Continental Cricket* (Hutchinson).

Every side has its behind the scenes workers and our team is no different. On the research side we must thank Olive Clark, A. G. Harfield, Derek Anns, Daniel Colman, Richard Edwards and Simon Holt for their work. We would also like to thank Simon Holt and Beryl Hill for their work on the manuscript.

Every effort has been made to trace the copyright holders of the materials used in this volume. Should there be any omissions in this respect, we apologise and shall be pleased to make the appropriate acknowledgements in future editions.

**You don't have to travel far from home to find some very rum goings on at the wicket. Malcolm Taylor's researches have unearthed as bizarre an episode in English cricket history as any tale from Borneo or Thailand.**

# Bring on the Clowns

'University of Cambridge beats Fourteen Clowns by an innings and 264 runs!'

This was the shock result beamed to the cricketing world on the morning of 14 August 1870. To be perfectly honest, a win for the University of Cambridge was probably anticipated even though (let's be honest again) the side was restricted to members of the Long Vacation Club. However, the margin of victory seems to have come as something of a surprise. At least the phenomenal scoring of the Cambridge Number Three was such as to earn him immortality in the pages of *Cricket Scores and Biographies*. To quote the Editor:

'This inferior match is inserted on account of the enormous [over 200] score made by Mr Scott, a curiosity, though against very inferior bowling and fielding.'

The quality of the fielding A. T. Scott, Esq., was up against as he hammered his way to a total of 202 run out (no complete Clown there!) is suggested by a contemporary illustration in *The Graphic*. Silly mid-off is about to turn a somersault. Extra-cover is standing on his head. Fine-leg is waving a policeman's baton. Square-leg is standing on one leg. Three silly mid-wicket fielders are falling over each other in a futile attempt to stop the ball.

But how, you may ask, did such an ill-matched fixture come about? The Editor of *Cricket Scores and Biographies* fills in a little of the background for us:

'It may here be mentioned that this was the second season of the Clowns' matches. Commencing in 1869, they have, under the leadership of the Clown Harry Croueste, played in various localities where their services as comical cricketers are appreciated and well paid, but not here recorded. Two, if not three, itinerant Clown Elevens now [1877] display, in various places, their curious antics.'

Looking at the first innings of the Fourteen Clowns and their humiliating follow-on at Fenner's it's difficult, at least at this distance in time, to see what could have been so richly diverting about Mr Charcoal's pair of spectacles, or Dan Rice's 'b Gordon o, b Scott o', though it's true Jolly Seal raises a statistical interest by scoring precisely three in both innings.

But then a scorecard can never fully convey the measure of a batsman's 'curious antics'.

Certainly we are looking at a period when the frontiers of 'showbiz' and cricket were a little blurred (you could say the same for our own times). After all, the first Australian touring team to England, operating around this period incidentally, was a party of Aborigines who in between overs entertained the spectators with exhibitions of boomerang throwing. This is also the era of the mutilated elevens. On 24 May 1872 at Ipswich a One-Legged Team sent their One-Armed opponents crashing to an innings defeat. 'The One-legged party won easily, having the advantage in the power of hitting' (*The Ipswich Journal*).

The problem for the selectors of the Clown Elevens must always have been how to strike a balance between demands of pure entertainment and the necessity of keeping a team of the calibre of the University of Cambridge Long Vacation Club in the field for at least half an afternoon. E. ('Ted') Peate, a professional cricketer of the period, reveals with some pathos how managements attempted to solve the problem:

'. . . They advertised for professional cricketers and I applied and was accepted. We finished our tour at Sheffield by getting well mobbed and sodded. The "grinders" saw no fun in booby cricket; they preferred the genuine article and gave us an emphatic reminder of the fact.

'The Company consisted of eight acrobats, eight talking clowns and eight cricketers. Of course I could do a bit of talking when I thought it necessary and I made one attempt to figure as an acrobat. It was at Newport Pagnell. One of our professional acrobats was exhibiting his dexterity in hanging downwards by the toes. I thought I would show how easy it was and attempted the same feat. Somehow the toes wouldn't stick and I fell to the ground on my head. I at once came to the conclusion that I was not a born acrobat.'

We have here a touching glimpse of a serious cricketer with ambitions to be a clown? Were there also clowns who longed to be Graces? On with the motley! *Cricket Scores and Biographies* has a brief portrait of a man who seems to have succeeded at being both – Arthur Thomas E. Treloar, formerly of Middlesex and more recently of 'some club in the West of England'.

Writes the Editor: 'Of late years he has travelled about the country as Captain and Manager of the so-called Imperial Clown Cricketers or Treloar's Clown Eleven; but none of their scores are admitted into these pages, nor the doings of the rival clowns. . . . Height 5 ft 8 ins and weight 10 st 10 lbs. Resides in London or at Torquay. In August 1876, he took a Clown Eleven to America, on speculation, which no doubt turned out very profitable.'

Is this the real reason why the Americans took up baseball?

MALCOLM TAYLOR

The Clowns XI visit to the Americas does not seem to have done any irreparable harm to Anglo/American relations. In 1886, for example, a Canadian team toured England and Ireland. The tourists' account we reproduce here does seem to dwell on social matters at the expense of the game itself. Yet even English tourists have sometimes been censured in this respect.

# Canadian Tourists

**Following on in Dublin**
All out for 88, and off went the carrier pigeons to the different newspaper offices to tell that Canada had to follow on.

These birds are much used by reporters to carry hourly messages from the cricket field to headquarters. The writing is fastened by an elastic band round the bird's ankle, then it is released. The first course is upwards, then it circles around once or oftener to get its bearings, mounts higher and goes direct to its destination. When several birds bound for different points are released at the same time, their airy circlings high above the field, their looking for home, and then their starts upon their different routes are beautiful to behold, and seem to impress you with the idea that there is something almost human about the movements of the winged messengers.

The Irish fielding was extremely good, and the bowling on the whole was good, though with the exception of Emerson's there was nothing particularly dangerous about it.

**Onwards to Hove**
We reached the grounds late, a breach of cricketing etiquette very unpardonable in England; but it was the train's fault, not ours. Who should be awaiting us but our 'Parson', Aston, to whom we hollered a salutation from the top of the drag. This Anglo-Saxon form of greeting dumbfounded a duchess-dowager spectator, who evidently thought that that sort of thing was done by us by rubbing noses in Ojibway, for she ejaculated in blank astonishment and in an audible voice, 'Why, I declare, they speak English!' This caused 'the Baby', Fleury, to laugh so immoderately that the venerable lady formed a mental estimate that even if we had learned to speak English we had not yet learned how to be polite, and relapsed into her seat, quite satisfied that she really knew all about the ways of the aborigines of the great North American Continent.

## At Lord's

When we had been transported in two breaks to the magnificent ground of the Marylebone Cricket Club, the famous 'Lord's', we found a large number of people waiting our appearance. A look at the ground revealed to us its great size, and its excellent appointments at once impressed us. On inquiry we learned that there was seating accommodation under cover for sixteen thousand people. It is, perhaps, needless to say that the pavilion and dining hall far surpass anything of the kind in England, and they have certainly been designed, not only with a view to convenience but to luxurious ease. Racket and tennis courts exist for those fond of good hard exercise.

The scoring apparatus is a most ingenious piece of mechanism, and enables a spectator at a glance to learn, after any run has been made, not only the total number of runs, the wickets down, and the last man's score, but also the individual scores of the two batsmen, which are increased run by run till a wicket falls.

The field looked level as a billiard table, and here, under as bright a sun as ever shone on old England, we were to play the most important match of our tour.

Little's wicket fell that night at 161, leaving the remaining three wickets, including Allan not out with 29, to get 69 on the morrow to save the follow-on.

But before we were to accomplish this we were to have the pleasure of dining in the pavilion as guests of the MCC. We were asked to sit down in mufti as it was a long way from the ground to the hotel and back. The Hon. E. Chandos Leigh, the President of the Marylebone Cricket Club in its centenary year, presided, supported on the left by Dr Ogden and on the right by Lindsey, on whose right sat Sir Henry Ponsonby Fane, the Lord Chamberlain. The Club's Secretary, Mr Perkins, occupied the vice-chair and on his left sat Mr Thomas Collins, the father of our own 'Dooks'.

The Chairman welcomed us to England as Canadians and as cricketers, and was kind enough to refer to our presence as an event of no small moment in the annals of the centenary year of the Marylebone Club. Our orators, the Captain and Manager, responded in fitting terms to the toast which some fifty gentlemen had done us the honor to drink. We then toasted our hosts and the opposing eleven, and accentuated the spirit of it by three rousing Canadian cheers.

After a response by Mr I. D. Walker, the captain of the MCC, some of the gentlemen retired, whereupon the evening grew frolicsome and songs and stories enlivened the proceedings until nearly midnight, when after a processional hymn to the tune of 'Marching back to Georgia', in which the Secretary took a leading part, we said good-night. It was particularly noticeable that our fellows who had attended St Paul's and Westminster Abbey the day before were in great form for this valedictory chant.

## In Grace Country

There is no hotel at this place, so we made arrangements to have our seventy-eight pieces of luggage, minus our cricket bags, sent on to

Weston-Super-Mud. As the fellows dived into their trunks for some of the wearing apparel that they needed, we were forcibly reminded of our arrival at Derry, when the same 'seventy-eight' ran the gauntlet of the Customs authorities. The 'General Manager' who had charge of the luggage was more forcible than polite in his language when he found that our traps would have to be piled up at the station to await another train, ere they could go on to their point of destination.

As Mr Chamberlayne was not aware of the hour at which we would arrive, we had to shoulder our knapsacks and march to the field of battle, at which we arrived tired out, dirty, and in the worst possible humour. The original arrangement had been to play the Gentlemen of Gloucester at Clifton, but this was subsequently altered to the match at Yatton. Mr Tankerville Chamberlayne, cricket's best patron in the famous County of Gloucester, had generously invited us to play his eleven of the same County, upon his private ground; a ground of which he may well be proud. Some eight acres had been enclosed by a high canvas wall, and a large luncheon and larger refreshment tents had been hoisted within the enclosure. Behind the neat little pavilion, in front of which we were photographed with the contesting team, a large dancing tent had been put up, where the villagers tripped the light fantastic at the conclusion of each day's play, to the music of the band which whooped it up for us in the afternoon. As the bandsmen had assembled on the ground before we got there, and bunting was flying from every available post, the whole scene bore a holiday aspect which was refreshing.

When the County of Gloucester plays with the first-class counties of England, seldom, if ever, do more than two professional players appear upon the Eleven; it is therefore, perhaps, in a position to put the strongest amateur county Eleven in England in the field. But the choosing of the team was not confined to Gloucester, for as Yatton is in Somersetshire, F. A. Smith, who is reported to be the hardest hitter in South Western England, made one of the team.

The Captain took Saunders with him to the wicket but came back without him at 34. Henry, Allan and Gillespie fell before the telegram had got much past the 60, and by the time 63 had been reported Saunders strode into the pavilion, having succumbed to Hale after making 29. This bowler and Pager did all the damage up to this point. George Jones and Little set about following the example which Saunders had set, and played so steadily that they brought on Dr E. M. Grace, whose brother caught Jones off one of his lobs, after he had made 23. Six for 116. Little, whose batting had steadily improved throughout the tour, did not lose his wicket, and saw all the rest out and 140 hoisted before he came in with 31 to his credit. Dr W. G. Grace was not successful with the ball, getting but one wicket at a cost of 61 runs, but his brother's lobs got him three wickets for 20.

The luncheon table, laden with the good things of this world, was graced by the presence of Mrs Grace and young W. G. Chamberlayne had spared no pains to give us a good lunch and he succeeded admirably; we were only sorry that he himself could not be present. An itinerant wasp stung Page on the tongue, which circumstances frightened the orators and constrained them to silence.

At four o'clock the two Graces commenced the innings for Gloucester, and we expected almost any amount of leather hunting. They kept up a running conversation while in together, and some of their remarks were very humorous, and on this occasion, as always, they put the large concourse of spectators in a good humour, to the merriment of whom George Jones added not a little in an early stage of the innings, by going head first over the ropes and upsetting a bench in a frantic attempt to save a boundary hit. Dr 'E.M.' retired at 49, just after his brother had given an impossible chance to Allan at the boundary. Henry, who was keeping wickets, had nipped up the retiring batsman. The next two wickets fell for next to nothing.

There had been a tennis party at 'Swiss Villa' in the afternoon, and there was to be a ball in the evening, and by the time those of us who were not quartered at Mr Cox's had assembled there the first dance was over. Here was a chance! The girls of England, of whose beauty and charms we had heard so much, we had hitherto met only in a casual way about the cricket fields, except at the evening at Mrs Colonel Bowlby's at Portsmouth; but now we were to have a jolly good dance with them. Though the evening was warm we went right in for it, and the way we waltzed through the programme that night calls back the time when, as school-boys, we used to start at No. 1 and keep it going till all the other guests but ourselves had said goodbye.

When the candles had burned low, and the approach of Sunday morning all too soon put an end to the festivities, the tender adieus showed what excellent use we had been making of our opportunities.

'TWO CRICKET VAGRANTS'

Ireland seems to receive only scant regard in the cricketing text books. The following story, however, illustrates the bitter nature of the Celtic experience. Indeed in the piece below we may perhaps discern the true origins of the Irish Question.

## Cromwellian Spoil-Sport

By the middle of that same seventeenth century, the game evidently enjoyed an enormous popularity in Ireland, for Cromwell ordered the destruction of all bats and balls in Dublin, and large numbers were given up for burning in 1656. Two hundred years later, the Irish were again found to have a strong love for the game: there seems to have been some kind of affinity for it amongst parts of what are loosely called the Celtic populations of the British islands.

ROWLAND BOWEN, *Cricket: a History of its*
*Growth and Development throughout the World*

> The Lord-Protector's attack on cricket in
> Ireland certainly seems to have had some
> sort of effect. It may well explain the prob-
> lems that Terence Prittie encountered
> when playing in a local derby match in
> Tipperary in the thirties.

## Short Wickets in Tipperary

A couple of years back I drove my car to Lord's and brought it in at the car-park entrance, off Elm Tree Road. I drove towards the car-park but found an attendant, in white coat, zig-zagging along in front of me. A polite toot, and he turned:

'You know, you might have someone run into you one day.'

'Ah, not at all – sure I'm well-known to those who bring their cars and I come from a place you've never heard of – Nenagh!'

It's my former home-town. We exchanged notes. They included thoughts about the 'revival' of cricket in Nenagh, County Tipperary, in 1930.

There had been efforts to introduce cricket into Nenagh in the 1880s and 1890s. The game languished, for lack of available opponents. *Some* cricket was played in Limerick, a little in Clonmel. But cricket in Ireland remained centred in the North and the Dublin area. Cricket, everywhere else, has had a sporadic existence.

Our family home was five miles south of Nenagh, on the road to nowhere – a chunk of wild, mountainy country lay to the south and east. My father organised our primitive 'home pitch' in 1929. In that year, we had home and away games with Nenagh, with a population of 3,000 of whom perhaps 30 to 40 had played cricket elsewhere, at school, university or in a job in the Dublin area. There were two survivors from the 1890s.

Our Kilboy home-side just won the first match. The return was at Nenagh. The town's football ground was used for this occasion, but the organisers were aware of their main problem. 'Football' in Nenagh meant rugger, and rugger grounds are liable to cut up in the Bog of Allen and the Irish south-west. This led to a proposition to my father, the captain of the Kilboy side, which was unusual, although probably not unique.

When we tossed-up, it was with *two* objects in view. There was, as always, a choice of innings. The second object was 'choice of pitch'. The management of the Nenagh side had shown admirable prescience; the whole ground was wringing wet, and a 'pitch' might barely last one innings. So there would be two.

We won. So, rather unfairly, we batted, and had choice of pitches as well. We batted steadily, and made just over 100. The innings was uneventful, save for the crowd of onlookers. As in one-day cricket in England today, they seemed to be mainly football enthusiasts, indicated by cries, brays and meaningless clapping. At least they refrained from even more meaningless singing. There was a lot of lively conversation; in front of the Tavern at Lord's there is virtually none today.

Nenagh began their innings on the 'other' pitch. I was keeping wicket and the first ball of the innings, pitched at a modest medium-pace just outside the off-stump, seemed to me to arrive like lightning. I was standing up, and it hit me in the chest unfairly early. I settled down to watch the ball, my attitude that of a Strudwick or a Taylor rather than of a Knott or Marsh.

Was the pitch too short? One will never know, but something else was amiss. The first Nenagh man was big and cumbersome. He blocked several balls, then played back with a very dead bat. Even so, he managed to hit his own wicket. The more prosperous of the two Nenagh chemists arrived and hit his wicket at once; he was a small man, and I was left marvelling at his achievement.

Number four came and went; unusually, he was caught in the slips, but I flinched as he played his stroke; it seemed to me he was more engaged with his own off-stump than the ball. The next man in hit his wicket so hard that the bails were sent flying past my head and a stump nearly bounced into my eye. Only then did I – largely out of a sense of self-preservation – ask for the next batsman to give me his bat. I measured the crease; it was the length of a bat, not of a bat and a half. By then, the Nenagh score was 8 for four wickets, and the match had already been lost and won.

It would be pleasant to add that Nenagh cricket took off from this improbable start, and that cricket flourishes there today. Sadly, it's not the case. Ireland has produced some good cricketers (think of Sir T. C. O'Brien, E. L. Kidd, Jack O'Connor and Patsy Hendren himself!) but too much of Ireland is governed by monsoon and marsh. And is cricket suited to the Irish character? The late President de Valera told me that rugger *was* – his only concession to foreign sport. Climate makes no concessions at all.

TERENCE PRITTIE

**Before we embark upon our long *vacance* on the continent let us examine a classic of cricket writing. A. A. Thomson's story of frustration and misinformation must strike a responsive chord with any one who has attempted to find out the close of play score in a hostile environment.**

# Ashes Regained

And if I suffered at Lord's, what of Headingley? Do you remember a film in which Naunton Wayne and the ever-lamented Basil Radford wandered round Europe, worrying in a delightfully ridiculous way about what was happening in the Test Match at Manchester? Like so many misfortunes that occur to other folk, it seemed funny at the time. I waited until the Manchester Test was safely over. (If I didn't have a heart attack when Australia finished at 35 for eight, I shall live to be a hundred.) That should have been good enough. Before the 1953 Leeds Test came along I was determined to stand no nonsense. I was going to visit romantic Austria and moonlit Venice, Bride of the Adriatic. Surely, after Wardle had taken four for 7, a man might be allowed to relax for a fortnight. What a fellow wants is to get away from the atom bomb, the cold war and the imminence of national bankruptcy; in short, all the dull routine of everyday life, and soak his soul in peace and beauty. Though, of course, it was difficult for the soul to be at rest, with Hutton suffering from fibrositis. . . .

I deliberately turned my back on my own country. All went well at first. The sea was calm, the journey across Belgium and Germany was full of interest, and there was pleasure, not to mention instruction, in seeing Turin, Milan and the long causeway that leads to Venice. . . . That first glimpse in the soft evening light of the Grand Canal has an enchantment that age cannot wither. Byron saw it. The Brownings saw it. The passenger in the gondola abreast of mine saw it, leaned forward to wonder at it and, as he did so, accidentally dropped his hat in the water.

He said, unexpectedly and rather loudly, that it was a fair cow, and this peculiar ejaculation, rather than any marked accent, stamped him as a citizen of the great Australian Commonwealth. When I retrieved his hat for him, we discovered that we were being paddled to the same hotel. He was an amiable companion and our relations from the beginning were extremely pleasant. I was determined not to be the first to mention the Test Match. He talked to me of mediaeval glass, the magic of San Marco and Ruskin's *Stones of Venice*. I talked to him about Bondi Beach, Chips

Rafferty and the ornithorhyncus or duck-gilled water-mole. I hope I appeared witty and nonchalant. It was hard work.

'Never mind,' I said to myself, 'I'll find an English paper tomorrow.'

But I was unlucky. The following day I searched Venice from the Bridge of Sighs to the Lido (pavilion end), without even finding out whether England had lost the toss. (I need not have worried about that. Hutton never won the toss that year.) My Australian friend, whose name was Martin, kept slipping away on the pretext of posting postcards or buying some Venetian glass to send to his wife, but he always came back without (I suspected) having found what he wanted. Before he left Venice he was beginning to have a haggard look. I had, I think, lost several pounds myself.

We came back from Italy to Austria by coach over the historic Brenner Pass. The majestic Dolomites were wreathed in clouds, and Martin and I were wrapped in silence. It was in the Customs shed at the frontier that I first saw an English newspaper. It was stuffed under the straps of a rucksack worn by a big bony citizen in the crowd in front of me. I had virtually to stand on my head to see it and what I saw played havoc with my blood-pressure.

'Feeling faint?' asked Martin considerately.

'If I can read upside down,' I murmured, 'Hutton has got a duck.'

'Ha-ha – I mean, sorry. You'd better have a stiff peg of slivowitz. That should pull you round.'

For the next four days my agony was less in extent but more concentrated. Hampered though we were by the ignorance of foreigners, we managed to ascertain the score once, or nearly once, a day. We had to fight for every paper just as England was fighting for every run. In Innsbruck I followed a respectable old gentleman the length of the famous Maria-Theresienstrasse under the impression that he was carrying the *Manchester Guardian* only to discover that he was really a German professor, flourishing the *Frankfurter Zeitung*.

(England 167, Australia 161 for three.) At the moment when we obtained the news, from a kindly American, who little knew how he was turning the dagger in my wound, that Australia had filched – you couldn't call it scored – 48 for the last wicket, we were standing in front of the great cathedral at Salzburg, listening to Mozart, a man whom, in my less agitated moments, I have always considered as good as Victor Trumper in his own line. We were actually hanging by a bit of wire in the hair-raising cable railway car five thousand feet above the Hungerburg plateau, like peas in a matchbox, when we learned, from a sympathetic fellow-pea, that England's fate hung equally in the balance. Hutton was out in the second innings, too, but Edrich and Compton, old campaigners both, were making a fight of it. But we never heard another word that day.

It was on the way home that Fate began to turn the screw. We set off on a long railway journey, through a corner of Germany, back to Austria, and then into Germany again. Leaving the train we boarded a steamer, like a Mississippi showboat, to sail between castled crags and vine-clad slopes along the poet's 'wide and winding Rhine'. It was while passing the notorious Lorelei rock that I learned that five English batsmen had been lured to their doom and that my beloved country was only about 70 runs on. Why did I ever leave home? I should never have strayed all this way from Headingley, much less from my own wireless set.

Martin slept well. I know I did not. The train roared through the darkness. It was three o'clock before I dozed off. When I woke we were at Cologne. I stumbled out sleepily on to a darkened platform. By some miracle there was a bookstall right in front of me and, what was more, an English paper. I flung the boy a mark (about one and eightpence) and bundled back into the train. What was this? There was only one event in contemporary English history which interested me, and I could find no mention of it. Our return journey had brought us in front of schedule. This was Thursday's paper. I had missed the result, which would have been published in Wednesday's. In quiet despair I tumbled asleep.

When the train stopped next, it was at Aix-la-Chapelle; now it was Martin's turn to forage for a newspaper. I watched him toddle down the windy platform, a flapping overcoat over his pyjamas. I watched him as he located the paper-trolley.

He laid his hand on the newspaper, but, before he could open it, a frolic wind snatched it from his grasp and whisked it, provokingly, exasperatingly, maddeningly along the tracks. As he dashed after it in frenzied pursuit, our train moved off, quietly but inexorably, towards Ostend. I suppose a draw is a fair result.

And of course, we did win at the Oval. I never saw Martin again. Such a nice fellow.

A. A. THOMSON, *Cricket my Happiness*

The Anglo–French Entente concerning the summer game could have become even closer. French domestic politics prevented this important tour from going ahead.

# Revolutionary Bowling

The Duke of Dorset was Ambassador in Paris at the time of the Outbreak of the French Revolution. In the summer of 1789 he asked the Duke of Leeds, then Foreign Secretary, for an assurance of goodwill from the British Government to France. The Duke of Leeds was himself a keen cricket lover and it appears that it was he who arranged for a tour of English cricketers to Paris by way of a 'goodwill' visit. It is commonly said that the tour had been arranged by the Duke of Dorset but though he was most probably the originator of the idea, he was in no position to make detailed arrangements at that particular time. At all events, the first encounter the Duke of Dorset had with the team was when he met it in Dover, himself fleeing from the Revolution. It was probably the first cricket tour to have been arranged for political reasons – it was certainly the first, but by no means the last, to be cancelled for such reasons.

The great unanswered question – unanswered because never apparently asked – is who were the team going to play? Were they to act as a 'circus', like Spalding's two baseball 'nines' who toured England in 1874, to split into two teams playing five-a-side? Surely it was not to play as a team the English residents in Paris for no more then than now could they have met the full English strength? What then of the French? Were the French players good enough to take on the team, or even good enough to make up two mixed elevens? If so, their names are not known to us, nor what happened to them; if these questions could be answered, a whole new vista of old cricket would open up.

ROWLAND BOWEN, *Cricket: a History of its
Growth and Development throughout the World*

'I will take up my position at Halle or, if he approaches from the Namur side, Waterloo.' – *The Duke of Wellington on being invited by the Duke of Richmond to participate in a cricket match in Brussels*

'Up guard and hook 'em!' 'It was a damned close run.' 'The finger of Providence was on me and I was given not out.' Running again through Wellington's famous quotes we are tempted to wonder if it was not a cricket match rather than a battle that was enacted on the field of Waterloo on 18 June 1815. In this connection it's significant that the Duke's first entry into the record books is as a representative of Leinster in a cricket match at Trinity College, Dublin. Our suspicions have been further roused by the discovery of the following match report:

# Waterloo Match

Napoleon won the toss at the skirmish at Quatre Bras, and mistakenly, in the view of many commentators, decided to give Wellington 'first use of the crease'. Possibly he was influenced by the early morning moisture which had seeped through the covers on to the wicket as a result of the heavy overnight rain. Or, conceivably, he hoped that his bowlers would be able to exploit the notorious Mont St Jean 'ridge'. As it was, he was to enable England's batsmen to become firmly entrenched by lunchtime.

In fairness to the Emperor it has to be admitted that his attack was not at full strength. Desertions to King Louis's 'cricket circus' and other commercially organised tours had robbed him of players of the quality of Marshal Berthier, Marshal Masena, Malcolm Marshall and Derek Underwood. Even so, Napoleon's handling of the attack was to betray a curious lack of grasp. The promising seamer and close-catcher Graham Grouchy was banished to the outfield to chew grass and Prussian gentians, while Lobau, whose accurate donkey drops could have proved devastating in the conditions, was only brought in after tea, and by that time even Blücher's Prussians had learned to use their feet.

Ney had bowled creditably enough on the 1812–13 winter tour of Russia. However there was to be no cloud cover to assist his medium-pace inswingers on the Waterloo wicket and it was obvious before the new ball was many overs old that he was taking a hammering. Yet time and again the ball was thrown to this wearying but eager workhorse (later to be severely disciplined by France's Test and County Cricket Board).

Meanwhile what of England? Wellington had been caught flashing at the Duchess of Richmond's bail and significant holes were to be torn in his middle order batsmen. The Duke of Orange's Nassau battalion went cheaply (run out all the way to Brussels) and shortly after lunch Sir William Ponsonby was to be stumped chasing a Chasseur down the leg side. This was surely the moment for the Emperor to set a close field to 'save the single'. Yet even a second class county batsman (Lord Uxbridge, Bucks) was permitted to bat on with a missing leg ('I'm hit, your Grace!' 'My god, you were plumb in front, Uxbridge!').

The sturdy Uxbridge's mishap was, of course, a dangerous blow for England's batsmen, because their whole strategy was dependent on the strength of their square legs. On the receipt of a D'erlon or a Milhaud bouncer they would abandon their guards and scuttle rapidly to the on-side to form themselves into impenetrable 'leg squares'. It was Bradman against Bodyline all over again, but this time there was to be no Jardine – only a *jardin* in front of the *Belle Alliance* tavern where the disheartened Emperor was to be seen quaffing brandy long before opening time. No wonder the Duke of Wellington was able to declare before stumps, 'It has been a damn nice thing, Creevey!' and later to enforce the follow on. However our German allies – for once, as *Wisden* records, to find themselves on a winning side – still claim that the scorecard should read:

'Buonaparte, N., c. Blücher b. Ülow o.'

Much later, in his senility, the Duke was to claim that the match was actually played at recreation grounds near Slough.

ALLEN SYNGE

# A Bit of a 'Stony' Wicket

*The Times* had quite a long article on sport in France which pointed out, with some disdain, that the highest score ever made by a French cricketer was 96. This was hardly surprising, it suggested, since most French cricket pitches were constructed of stone. 'The public in France takes no interest in cricket, of which it does not understand the subtleties. The Frenchman grows impatient at waiting his turn to go in, and would like either to be batting or bowling the whole time. In a word, cricket is not sympathetic to the French temperament. There are scarcely a dozen Frenchmen who play cricket, and most of them play it abominably.'

TIM MATTHEWS

The First World War bought an army of cricketers to French soil. Germany was decisively beaten, but the French remained strangely unimpressed.

# Trench Cricket

It was a great game, we won of course, and Roger Rum got a blob, bless him. Anyway I won ten bob, and Johnny did love it. Small wonder, too, as he had actually registered more'n forty on the tins before he had his middle ash rather badly bent, watching 'em like the meanest private watches dear Minnie at Spanbroekmolen and connecting every time too he was. What an innings, in other words the real bons. As for the Editor, he revelled in it – he is rather roguish with the crimson rambler. Was I there? Search me as they say in Horace, and I may tell you that the day before when the Editor was batting I removed all three pegs with the second ball (the only reason it wasn't the first was because I'd previously arranged to let him get a couple by serving up a full toss well outside the crux peg providing he did the same to me when I staggered into the centre) well, as I've said, the Editor got a couple and then went out – quick – and during the remainder of the innings proceeded to prop up the bar at the regimental canteen during closed hours too – the horrid florid Forester! By the time, therefore, I took my stand he'd forgotten all about our little do, and hanged if the very first time he swung the spheroid at me it wasn't accompanied by a fearful crash of ash. He's no sportsman as you may or may not know, but I'm getting a trifle off the rails so I'll continue. The Professor turned up for a moment, and we assured him we weren't playing too much cricket but merely combining same with a little bombing practice. And what about our sometime Rugger international? I don't care to tell you how many he got as he's my CO so ask the Editor if you want the news. The wicket was as beautiful as Tina, and we had a priceless day although Bobbie wasn't playing.

'P.B.I.', *Somme Times*

The scene: the Parc des Princes, a February evening, twenty-eight Englishmen, SHAPE Headquarters and French politics. Missionary work continues.

## Floodlights, Waiters and a White Ball

Cricket was not in my immediate thoughts on that freezing February day thirteen years ago. True, I had just counted the weeks till the start of the next season, but the bat and ball seemed very far away as I watched snow settling on the window-sill of my office.

The fascination of a journalist's life is that the next 'phone call may be about anything from a Cabinet crisis to a weather report. Nothing so dramatic as the first came when I answered the tinkling bell on my office desk. Instead, the voice of a friend from Agence France Presse.

'Can you raise a cricket team for me by next Monday?' I looked out at the snow, asked him to repeat the request and finally spluttered: 'What the devil are you talking about?'

'No, I haven't been drinking,' came the reply. He had received a request from his head office in Paris enquiring whether an English side could be got together within the next three days to play an exhibition match there.

It was all rather obscure but I was told that a M. Maurice Gardet, an impresario with ambitions of getting into Parliament, had a novel idea of 'selling' cricket to the French people as part of his election platform. The story was that he had undertaken to pay the whole cost of an exhibition game between the Supreme Headquarters Allied Powers in Europe cricket side in France and a team specially brought over from England. The game was to be played under floodlights on the Parc des Princes stadium, Paris, on Monday evening. It was now after five p.m. on Thursday. Although suspicious that it was a gigantic leg-pull, I promised I would go ahead.

At eleven o'clock the following morning, a short, bearded figure bounded into my office. Breathlessly he announced, 'I am Maurice Gardet, I have just arrived from Paris. Can I have the names of your team?'

Almost before I had time to tell him that I had not contacted any prospective players, the telephone bell rang. He was wanted by Paris. SHAPE was caught up in something vitally important and couldn't raise a side. That did not worry Gardet.

'In that case, you must bring two teams,' he decided.

As patiently as I could, I explained that a cricket match required more than twenty-two players.

'It doesn't matter, bring whatever are necessary,' said Gardet. 'I will ring you from Paris tomorrow morning (Saturday) and give you your travel arrangements. How many will there be?'

The opportunity was too good to miss. 'Twenty-two players, two umpires, two scorers and' – my greatest ploy – 'two baggage men.' I would be one up on MCC. They only took one baggage man for a six-months' tour – and he did the scoring as well.

Nothing perturbed Gardet. Everything was easy, for him. Not quite so easy for me. Between midday on Friday and that evening I had to find a party of twenty-eight who would stage a cricket match, had – or could get – passports, and could escape from business for the best part of two days.

There was only one way to tackle this – an all-out assault by telephone. So to the first call.

'Roger, can you get Monday off?'

'Why?'

'I want you to play for me.'

'Play for you? What at?'

'Cricket.'

'Cricket? You're barmy! Have you been on the bottle?'

'No. I'm serious.'

'Look, stop wasting my time – I'm busy. What's this all about? Where is it?'

'In Paris.'

Hilarious laughter greeted this statement.

One by one, I persuaded cricketing friends to meet me at the Café Royal on Monday evening at 6.30, complete with cricket-bags and up-to-date passports. These included the then England captain, Ted Dexter, and the wicket-keeper, Godfrey Evans, a number of other county cricketers, one or two cricketing journalists and players from my own club.

On Saturday morning the Passport Office in Petty France was raided by a variety of disbelievers. On Saturday morning, too, M. Gardet telephoned me at home to say that twenty-eight seats had been booked on a plane leaving London Airport at midnight on Monday.

'You'll have to make us a special tie, of course,' I told him. 'Cricketers always expect a tie to signalise an outstanding occasion.'

'That will be no trouble, my friend,' countered the buoyant Gardet.

On Sunday, three French newspapers rang me for information about the English cricketers and Gardet himself was also back on the phone. The ties had been designed and were already in the process of manufacture; full arrangements had been made for our entertainment and he himself would head the reception committee at Orly Airport.

Snow was falling outside the following night when we gathered at the Café Royal. In the warmth of the bar, twenty-eight widely-assorted characters quickly caught the escapist feeling of the evening. All the time I parried the question: 'When do we leave?'

By ten p.m., however, most had decided it was a gigantic hoax. Never mind, they'd had a laugh together but they ought to be on their way home.

'All right,' I said. 'Follow me.' Down the carpeted stairs of the Café Royal we tumbled. At the foot, I fulfilled an ambition by asking an astonished commissionaire to get me eight taxi-cabs.

Into these we piled. 'London Airport the next stop.'

Some still wouldn't believe me. They only did so when they were on the plane – some making their first air-trip. Those who had discreetly placed liquid refreshment in their cases helped to maintain the spirit of the occasion during the hour's flight to Paris. There, true to his word, was the organiser.

'What have you lined up for us?' we clamoured to Gardet – after telephone, radio and television interviews had been concluded.

'Everything is organised. Don't worry: follow me,' announced Gardet. It was organised, too. We were taken to a night club. The only drink offered us there was champagne, lots of it. Not surprising that the floor-show went on in a noise not dissimilar to that of a Rugby club bar.

All good things come to an end. Our good things finished at four a.m. But, suddenly, everyone was overwhelmed by the same craving – hunger.

'Leave it to me,' said Gardet.

Taxis again down to Les Halles. Over some abattoir where the restaurant lights glittered invitingly piled the party. Menu cards were thrust into our faces and at once the ordering began – no one had forgotten it was 'all on the house'.

Oysters, smoked salmon, river trout, steak, mushrooms and tomatoes, chips – the orders were being given and taken with great relish.

'Stop, I have already ordered for you,' beamed Gardet. 'I have ordered the speciality of France.' Mouths watering, we waited, ten, fifteen minutes. Then out came the waiters . . . bearing twenty-eight bowls of thick, onion soup, covered in cheese – or was it blotting paper? Never mind, we hadn't the heart to register our disappointment. Instead we made that the hors-d'oeuvre. Afterwards, we scattered our various ways and in various groups. Ted Dexter, Godfrey Evans, John Warr and myself were eating escalope of veal at 6.30 a.m. Others dined even later. Some did not dine. But none arrived at the hotel allocated until 7.30 a.m. In the next hour, all checked in and fell into bed, either fully clothed or fully stripped.

At a quarter to nine my telephone rang. It was Gardet. 'The coach will be there for you at nine o'clock,' he announced. 'What coach?' I demanded.

'We have arranged a sight-seeing tour of Paris for you, starting off with wine-tasting in the vaults near the Eiffel Tower.'

Ten minutes later a waiter arrived, complete with breakfast and a further instruction from Gardet that we must not keep the coach driver waiting.

Sleepy-eyed, we crept aboard the coach and were soon deposited at the vaults, where we were taken underground for a long mazy walk before being invited to taste the wine of the country. Once again, the brew was Freeman's. Next came a trip up the River Seine followed by lunch in the restaurant of the Eiffel Tower several hundred feet above ground.

We were invited to make a tour of the shops to buy presents, but Ted Dexter and Godfrey Evans had a conscience about inspecting the playing conditions for the evening match. While the rest explored the Paris arcades, the two England cricketers visited the ground where, we had been told, a magnificent cricket pitch awaited our delectation. To their horror, they found it was a rough football ground on which any attempt at cricket would have been a hazardous adventure for batsmen, bowlers and fielders alike. In an instant, they were off to the SHAPE headquarters, where they borrowed a coconut mat the length of a cricket pitch, went back to the ground and laid it themselves.

Meanwhile, with shopping over, the remainder of the party gathered at the meeting place, clambered aboard the coach and set off for the ground. What was all that noise outside? The important visitors had been provided with an escort of motor cyclists playing fiercely on their klaxons.

Through the streets of Paris we proceeded to the ground, which was encircled by police and armed soldiers. Then into the dressing-rooms to change for 'Le Cricket', as it was widely advertised on the hoardings. The weather was decently mild and we decided only one sweater each would be necessary – that is, apart from two sets of underclothes. As we changed six waiters, resplendent in morning dress, marched sedately in line and in step, bearing huge silver tea-trays, complete with silver urns, jugs, the lot. Yes, the Englishman had to have his cup of tea.

Finally came the call to cricket. Gardet explained the procedure. 'You will proceed to the entrance to the pitch, line up in your two teams and run on to the field, where you will form up in one line.' Leeds and Liverpool at the previous year's Cup Final had nothing on us.

We did as we were told. As the two national anthems were played a beautiful girl appeared, acknowledged the wolf-whistles and threw us the ball for the match to begin. She was a French film actress – we never learned her name.

A ball? Yes – but a white hockey ball. We played for an hour each. Photographers crouched all over the field. They swarmed into action when one man was struck a blow over the eye and led off, bleeding profusely. For most of the spectators, this made the evening. They had seen that 'Le Cricket' was, after all, a man's game.

But many had fears for their own safety as, time after time, Dexter or Evans or another big hitter sent the ball flying into the stand, out of vision of the floodlights. 'Stop it! Stop it! Someone will get killed,' were the cries. But, for us, it was all good fun, especially when we were being interviewed for the radio between overs on the field.

We did play fairly seriously as we had considerable regard for M. Gardet, especially as he had told us that, apart from using cricket as an election appeal, he had decided to buy a village and to rename it 'Cricketville'. Especially, too, seeing that on our short coach journey from the vaults to the River Seine he had proved his unflappability when, in answer to his query, 'Is there anything you want?' we had told him, 'Alka Seltzers.' He had stopped the coach within seconds and came back immediately with six dozen bottles of the stuff.

After the match, the inevitable party. A party . . . It was held in a huge pavilion under the stand. After three hours of abundant hospitality I committed the one faux pas of the tour for which I have still not been forgiven. We were invited to stay another night instead of returning, as arranged, by plane that night. Regard for reputations, moral cowardice, fear of retribution, I don't know what it was, but I decided we must go back. As it turned out, it was probably for the best as, an hour after we had left Orly Airport, the fog closed in and not one plane left there for another three days. Some were speechless at my insistence on going home. Some were just speechless. It is on record that one – who had to be carried through the customs and whose name we signed as Malinovski – did not murmur again until three o'clock the following afternoon.

The ties? Each was presented with a green cloth tie on which the Eiffel Tower and a set of cricket stumps had been blazoned. We were also given two huge silver cups, specially struck, half a dozen flags and presents for the ladies.

Four days later my club, Stanmore, held their annual dinner at Lord's. Halfway through the meal a little Frenchman marched in. M. Gardet had flown over specially to reiterate his thanks.

The sequel? I just don't know. If M. Gardet is still around, I am one of twenty-eight people hoping to hear from him again. . . .

R. J. HAYTER, *The Cricketer*, January 1979

*Wisden* gave us the bare outline of Australia's match against Holland at The Hague in 1964. Further details were quickly provided by the champions of continental cricket, P. C. G. Labouchere, T. A. J. Provis and Peter S. Hargreaves.

# How to Beat Australia: an Eyewitness Account

The scene of this sensational event in the cricket world was the ground of the Haagsche Cricket Club, which in winter is used for football. It is small and snug with two little covered stands, willow trees, a brightly-painted pavilion set off with a terrace in front of it, with the dressing-rooms behind a rose garden, and flags flying and deck-chairs in hundreds around the boundary.

More than three thousand cricket followers were gathered here to see these Australian players whose deeds in England had been heard by tuning in to the BBC Third Programme, and the names of McKenzie, Booth, O'Neill or Burge were very familiar to many of the Dutchmen who watched. Most of the time the sun shone, with a couple of very light showers alone reminding those present that the country possessed what is euphemistically called a 'sea climate'.

The All Holland side was without its best spinner and all-rounder, Nico Spits, who, as a member of the Olympic hockey team selected for Tokyo, had to attend a match against Great Britain the same day. This clash of these two sporting events might also have influenced their respective attendances. Of the eleven that had opposed the Australians on the same ground in 1953, Wally van Weelde, Ernst Vriens and Peter van Arkel were again appearing. On the other hand all of the touring Australian team were new to Dutch cricket. In 1953 Vriens had taken the wickets of Harvey, Benaud, Archer and Ring for 85 runs, while van Arkel – then a mere lad of 17 – had top-scored for Holland with a fine 34 against an attack consisting of Archer, Davidson, Ring and Benaud. For the Australians on the present occasion Brian Booth captained the side because Bobby Simpson had injured a finger, and after winning the toss he elected to take first use of the wicket.

Lawry and Grout started confidently against an opening attack which was not very impressive, but then, at 15, Lawry glanced a ball to leg-slip for veteran Wally van Weelde to take a brilliant catch a few inches above the ground. A good ball from Trijzelaar then sent Grout back at 36, and at this stage O'Neill and Burge decided to take a good look at the bowling because both Pierhagen (left-arm medium) and Vriens (right-arm medium) were operating too well on the matting to be taken lightly. Burge was never really comfortable, though, and in the course of one maiden Pierhagen beat him twice all ends up without succeeding in getting an edge or hitting the stumps. After being dropped when on 15, O'Neill played attractive cricket, chiefly with hooks and square-cuts, but it was noticeable that the visitors showed little inclination to attack on the front foot, possibly through finding the sharp rise of the ball from the matting to be a risky proposition for straight or cover drives.

Booth was well caught on the boundary while attempting a big hit. Several spectators doubted if the catch was in order, for the fielder, Bouwman, stepped over the line, but Booth walked without question. Potter then had the misfortune to mistime a rising ball from the fast-bowler Trijzelaar and be hit on the head. He had to be taken to hospital at once, where he was discovered to have sustained a slight fracture of the skull.

After a shower of rain interrupting play for about ten minutes, O'Neill then set about the bowling and was finally stumped soon after lunch by Schoonheim for what had been an attractive 87, made in 110 minutes. The remaining batsmen offered little resistance against some accurate bowling and very keen fielding, and the innings closed for 197 – somewhat disappointing on this small ground considering that the 'Aussies' of eleven years before had made 279 here (Morris getting 70 and McDonald 66). No one of the 3,000 or more spectators here had even so much as entertained the thought of a possible Dutch victory, however, for All Holland had never been permitted to make more than 130 up to that time by a touring side, and had generally been dismissed for rather less than even that modest total.

The openers Marseille (who had a hundred against Hampshire to his credit two years earlier) and van der Vegt (a newcomer) survived the first onslaught, however, even if the latter took a long time to get off the mark. But when they were well set a shower then interrupted play, meaning that they had to begin their task again. This proved to be to their favour, because the Australians were unable to use their long studs on the matting and had to bowl and field in rubbers – something which certainly prevented a man like McKenzie from bowling full out.

With the first wicket not falling until 99 runs were on the board after 90 minutes' play, it must then have been fully clear to Booth that this game was not going to be a mere exhibition. Marseille's sound 77 and the plucky 33 of van der Vegt had supplied a sturdy foundation to the innings, in fact, and it was up to the skipper, van Arkel, to try to drive home the advantage. Following a very uncomfortable first over from McKenzie he proceeded to do this in excellent style, making good use of his great height and giving a fine display of timing. After he left, though, 50 runs still had to be made in 40 minutes, and with McKenzie and Cowper bowling at their best at that stage the most that Holland expected was a well-merited draw. The powerful forcing batsman, Wally van Weelde, did not last long, much to the audible disappointment of the crowd, for in having announced his intention of retiring from international cricket this was his last All Holland match. Two more wickets also fell quickly, which did not improve the position at all.

One man who thought otherwise of the situation, however, was Rudi Onstein – a batsman with a very vulnerable defence but a match-winner par excellence on certain occasions when things look black. When at last seventeen runs were needed to win, with a bare three overs' play left, Onstein drove Cowper for six. At this point he and his team-mate, Wijkhuizen, took two lightning singles, and could well have been described as scutting like rabbits – appropriately, considering what damage those animals also have done to Australia in the past. Then, in the midst of noticeable tension all round, a maiden was bowled to Wijhuizen by McKenzie, and when the last over was announced nine were needed to win. Two extremely risky singles followed, and another ball soaring over the sightscreen brought the scores level: and then the fourth ball of the over was hooked for a four, and Holland achieved the seemingly impossible and played herself on to the map of the cricketing world!

The scene which followed was without parallel in the history of Dutch cricket. Even before the ball reached the boundary a roar was on its way up from 3,000 throats, and hats were flung into the air as hundreds of people ran out on to the field to try to pat the players on the shoulder – or, failing that, each other – while women giggled nervously or shed abundant tears. The Australians also received their share of back-slapping, for it had certainly been realised by the crowd how comparatively easy it could have been for Brian Booth to adopt defensive tactics during those last forty minutes in order to save the game. Instead he had chosen to play for a win, with McKenzie attacking as hard as he was able and Cowper tempting the batsmen at the other end to fall into error in the course of their haste. In doing this, Booth received the gratitude of all who had watched, for his action had resulted in what must have been one of the most thrilling matches – and undoubtedly the most sensational – seen in their lives.

P. C. G. LABOUCHERE, T. A. J. PROVIS AND P. S. HARGREAVES,
*The Story of Continental Cricket*

It would appear that we are partly in-
debted to Adolf Hitler for the popularity
of the game in Holland and Denmark, for
while he temporarily stopped play, he was
to be indirectly responsible for a cricketing renaissance.

## Hitler Stopped Play

The fact that Germany was defeated, the fact that cricket is
an English game (or is thought to be), the fact that the troops liberating
both Holland and Denmark were British have all contrived to make the
game there far more popular than it was. In both countries, right up to the
time of the rise of Hitler (and even after in respect of a very small
minority), there had been large sections of the community who admired
Germany and German culture. It was often said that Dutchmen aspired to
the ways and clothes of either a German junker, or of an English country
gentleman: the war removed one choice entirely, and cricket has be-
nefited accordingly: lately for the first time, there has been some possibility of the game being played in Dutch and Danish schools, on which a
useful comment is to note the assiduity with which cricketers in both
countries have always brought on their young, knowing that if the seed can
be planted, the game is safe.

ROWLAND BOWEN, *Cricket: a History of its*
*Growth and Development throughout the World*

How many games require the offer of a
thousand cigarettes and a second-hand
German lorry before the opening pair
walk to the wicket? A correspondent from
*The Times* gives us a flavour of post-war
Dutch cricket.

## Blackmarket Balls

The 'appalling shortage of playing gear' in Holland is due to
the fact that the Dutch collected all available cricket gear in Holland and
dispatched it to British prisoner-of-war camps in Germany.
I can personally testify to the shortage, as I had the honour to captain
the first British eleven to play against a 'Free Dutch' side ten days after the
liberation of The Hague; our opponents were our old friends The Hague

Cricket Club. After all our combined attempts to obtain a cricket ball had failed, a highly polished hockey ball was used. The enormous inducement of a thousand cigarettes and one German lorry failed to bring forth even an old or worn cricket ball. The Hague scored 70, while we were all out for 17. We did not blame the hockey ball, the patchwork matting, or the 3½-hour lunch.

R. H. MACDONALD, letter to *The Times*, 2 January 1946

**The relationships between cricketing nations have had their hiccups over the years. Bodyline in Australia, Jackman in the West Indies and Fletcher in India are three such events. They could have been joined by the Flamingos at Lord's if it had not been for the language barrier.**

## Language Barrier

On one occasion, the whole relationship between the cricket of Holland and the MCC was actually saved from what might have proved to be irreparable consequences through the total lack of knowledge of the language of the Dutch visitors by the home side of Lord's itself. The Flamingos' team had made 158, and with the home side with 141 on the board when their ninth wicket fell it appeared that the Dutchmen were about to achieve their first ever victory at headquarters. Number eleven was thought to be a 'rabbit', although at the other end was none other than one of the great figures of English cricket of all time – but whose name we might spare mentioning in this instance. Number eleven received his first ball which was a half-volley, but perfectly straight, and after missing it with an almighty swipe he stopped it with both legs plumb in front of his middle stump. Eleven Dutchmen then appealed like one sole man, with the thought that their finest hour had struck – but the umpire's reactions were peculiar. Slowly he raised his arm with finger outstretched, but the sudden sight of the certain great English cricketer at his side seemed to send a chill through him. Shaking his head, he lowered both finger and the arm, to say sadly, 'Not out.' A few minutes later the great English cricketer scored the winning run, and eleven Flamingos left the field in the silence of perfect discipline, broken only by some sympathetic cries from the Members' Pavilion of 'Hard luck, sir!' and 'It's all in the game. . . .'

The great English cricketer sensed that the situation was not the best for the enjoyment of a carefree drink at the bar at this stage, though, and as captain of the MCC side he suggested that the visitors might bat again in the hour left for play 'to please the crowd' – which numbered a good 300, with the ground staff and the boys selling the scorecards included. When the Flamingos' skipper entered his side's dressing-room to break the news, he found half of his team already under the showers, and the others in various stages of undress arguing in no mild phrases or temper. He at length succeeded in getting his opening pair dressed again and padded, and told them in equally strong terms to shut their mouths and get out to where they were awaited. When the number one looked up to take guard, however, he was no little embarrassed to find himself confronted by the umpire of the drama, and the latter asked him what he wanted.

'Middle, you —,' said the batsman, using a word in his own language that, if known to any of the others on the field save his partner, might have put the first nail into a coffin for Anglo–Dutch cricketing relations. Moreover, he then proceeded to let off steam by scoring about 40 in ten minutes, and in less than an hour's time with the total at 74 or so the tension had died down sufficiently for tankards to be enjoyed with better digestion!

P. C. G. LABOUCHERE, T. A. J. PROVIS AND P. S. HARGREAVES,
*The Story of Continental Cricket*

The season of 1930 was nearing its end. As Bradman and Ponsford continued to put the Counties' bowling to the sword, another party of tourists set diffident feet on these shores. Germany was seeking to further 'détente' through the medium of bat and ball. As the leading authority on German cricket tells us, these white flannelled doves were to encounter a mixed reception.

# England Tour, 1930

Many Germans wounded in the Great War had been nursed at the Lower Southern Hospital, Dartford, and it was appropriate that the opening match should have been against the local Club on the emotive date of 4 August. This visit to Dartford did not pass off without some controversial correspondence in the *Dartford Gazette* and *Kentish Times*. Under the heading 'August 4, 1914' a Rosemary Britain wrote to the Editor: 'I understand that August 4th, 1914, is to be commemorated in Dartford next Monday by giving a civil welcome to a German cricket team. What a delightful way of remembering. Might I suggest as an addition that the name of the town be changed to "Dhartfordt", and that at least some of the townsmen who were prisoners of war in Germany for years should perform the re-christening ceremony.' Mr A. Spence Boyse, however, asked the lady if she was 'aware that peace has been made with Germany? Or does she fail to realise that "peace" – real peace – means more than the mere cessation of active hostilities?' He continued to draw analogies, mentioning the Altar of Baal, Carthage, Cato, Hannibal and the Dark Ages. Mr T. Hill referred to Rosemary Britain as 'evidently one of the few chauvinists left' and deplored that we learn nothing from history, each war becoming more ghastly than the last. 'Her suggestion that Dartford be re-named Dhartfordt is, I am afraid, unnecessary,' closed Mr Hill. 'If she will refer to the dictionary she will find that the word "Ford" is Anglo-Saxon! The inference is obvious.'

The team arrived in London on the evening of Friday 1 August. On Sunday they attended services at St Paul's Cathedral and Westminster Abbey; and on the Monday were received in a spirit of good fellowship at Hesketh Park by members and friends of Dartford CC. Within half-an-hour the Germans were changed and practising for the very first time on a turf wicket, looking smart in their blue blazers, emblazoned with a bear rampant in red, and their white caps. The scene was shot by photographers, 'movie' and 'talkie' men, for British, German and American audiences.

Bowling and fielding revealed the tourists' strengths: unaccustomed to turf wickets – soft after the rain – they showed they had much to learn. It was the later batsmen who scored most runs, after an early collapse. Schmidt, at number nine, caused much amusement by the disdainful manner in which he treated balls not quite to his liking, allowing them to hit his portly person in the most unconcerned way and hoping for leg-byes. When he decided to hit, however, he put everything into his stroke, and was rewarded with one mighty six. The best innings was played by Thamer at number eleven: his was much the straightest bat.

*The Bedfordshire Standard* committed a rather amusing error over Kirloskar. After commenting that the tourists seemed 'very pleasant, sociable fellows . . . with a useful working knowledge of English', they continued: 'One in particular with whom it was possible to carry on quite an animated conversation on sport was W. Kirloskar, keen-eyed and sun-tanned, the best all-rounder in the team . . . There was little of the traditional Teutonic phlegm about this young gentleman, whose vivacity suggested rather the Latin type.' Evidently, the reporter was unaware that his subject hailed from the Bombay Presidency!

As it was, there was some real embarrassment caused at the outset, the tourists having run into some matters of protocol at The Oval. The *Daily Mail* of 4 August ran such banner headlines as GERMAN TOURISTS' COLD WELCOME and SURREY REFUSE THEM SEATS. The paper reported that 'the team of German cricketers visited the Oval on Saturday' (2 August) but added that 'their application to be allowed seats in the Pavilion was refused. Many people on the ground who heard of the incident were indignant that the same courtesy which continental clubs extend to visiting British teams was denied to the Germans. . . .'

R. C. N. Palairet, Secretary of the Club, wrote to 'G. Henderson, organiser', about the matter under the date 4 August, and the text of the letter was released to the Press. It read as follows:

Dear Sir,

I see it stated in the newspaper that the eleven from Germany who are visiting this country asked for and were refused admission to the Pavilion at the Oval on Saturday last.

These are the facts. At about 12.30 p.m. on Saturday a verbal message was brought to me which I understood to be that a man was below asking if any privileges had been granted to the German eleven for the Test Match. [Surrey were playing Nottinghamshire at the time.] To this my reply was 'No', no privileges having been asked for.

If I had realised that all the members of the team were present and were asking for admission for the day, I should at once have arranged for their admission, this being the usual practice at the Oval.

I trust you will convey to the members of the German eleven my sincere apologies for the quite unintentional slight offered to them.

Yours faithfully,
R. C. N. PALAIRET

It was a question of poor public relations work on each side, related to a language problem. As it was, the tourists re-visited the Oval on 11 August as guests at lunch of the President of Surrey, H. D. G. Leveson Gower, and watched the County play Middlesex from a point of vantage on the Stand.

JAMES D. COLDHAM, *German Cricket*

# Dartford in Berlin, 1931

Invited to visit Berlin for a short time in the following year, Dartford CC gave a bannerette to Herr P. Faber, President of the Berlin Cricket League, for eventual presentation to the winner of the League in 1931 and future years. At a banquet at the Russian Hotel, Faber complimented the visitors on their interpretation of the 'Spirit of Cricket'. Repeated requests were made for the Dartford men to come again; and a party of the Germans, on the team's departure, handed – with a bunch of roses – a card on which the message read:

Take these roses home with you:
Flowers, alas, must perish,
But the thoughts which go with them
May you ever cherish.

JAMES D. COLDHAM, *German Cricket*

The late lamented Terence Prittie did
much for the spread of cricket in many
parts of the globe. But here we find him
embarked on a mission impossible, or
very nearly – the conversion of the Hitler
Youth to the game.

# Are the English Sadists?

When I left school my parents, after much debate, decided
that I should use at least four of the eight months to run before going up to
Oxford in learning a foreign language. And my father decided that the
language should be German; he remained convinced to the day of his
death that the French had charged us rent for the use of the trenches in
the Great War. To Germany I went, to the South German town of
Freiburg-in-Breisgau. It had a University, a blackcloth of lovely hills and
forests, and a remarkably peaceful atmosphere. For this was May 1933
and Adolf Hitler had just come to power.

I stayed with an 'army family', decent, friendly folk who were in
something of a whirl over the sudden change in German history. It left the
family divided and, for the first time in many generations, without an elder
son going into the Army. The father was a staunch conservative, but no
longer with a political party which he could vote for. The mother was
concerned only with children, church and kitchen, all spelt with a 'k' in
German.

The 21-year-old elder son was anti-Nazi and had gone to work in
Konstanz, and I saw little of him. The 18-year-old daughter was a
fanatical Nazi, and the second son, two years younger, was rapidly being
converted to the same creed. The children regarded me with some
suspicion, for 'der Führer' kept sounding off about the sins of the British
Press.

I had brought golf-clubs with me, unaware that the only course within
fifty miles was at Baden-Baden and that its green fees would have been far
beyond the scope of my modest allowance. More bizarre was the fact that I
had also brought cricket gear; I had fondly imagined that at least *some* of
the inhabitants of Freiburg played the game. My accoutrements were
regarded by all the members of the family with amazement, tinged with
mirth.

I was first interrogated (the Germans are born interrogators!) about the
golf-clubs. Why did I have so many, instead of one? Why were they 'the
wrong way round', in fact left-handed? For golf-clubs *had* been seen in
Freiburg, although not in this particular household's possession. Would I
show them how the clubs worked?

I took out a ball and a club – in those far-off days it was labelled
'mashie'. We went on to the lawn and I did a few chips which impressed
nobody. Was that all that I could do? I told them that I could, if necessary,

hit the ball over their house. This was greeted with ribald laughter. Bets were taken, and I teed-up. The mother had stationed herself, protectively, in front of the drawing-room windows.

The ball sailed well over the roof – there was, after all, only one upper story – and landed in a small park on the other side. No one was injured and bets were paid with an ill grace. I was made to feel that I had taken advantage of my prior knowledge.

Next my cricket gear came in for inspection, and a new interrogation began. Ludicrously, I had brought full batting equipment, two balls and a set of stumps. These were all fingered, with one exception; I had put my box away, for I felt a truthful answer about it would simply not be believed.

The elder son was back for the weekend and all three German young wanted to see how the game was played. But the lawn was not the place for this. It was a dampish day in late May and the lawn was mossy and partly water-logged. Germans rarely master the art of making a reasonable lawn. So we walked to a piece of waste ground half a mile away on the edge of the town. The elder son walked with me. Sigrid and Gunther sang Nazi marching songs.

The stumps were set up and Gunther insisted on batting first. I had shown him how to use a bat, and he struck an aggressive posture, like Graham Gooch, holding his bat above his head. I bowled him a very slow lob.

By pure luck he struck it away into some bushes, then collapsed with laughter. Was this all that the game of cricket was about? Why, it was ridiculously easy! He would strike the next ball in exactly the same way! The Germans would beat the English at their own game!

I was a wicket-keeper, but I could bowl a little, so I served up the ball over-arm, at a fair medium-pace. It struck Gunther on the knee-cap, and he had refused to put on pads. He fell to the ground, hurling the bat away and howling with pain.

I was upbraided by all three of them. I had struck Gunther on purpose and out of anger because he had hit the ball away the previous time! I had probably cheated, for my arm had come up almost to my head! Even the elder son, Max, was disgusted: 'Are the English sadists?' he asked me. 'Otherwise why do you invent a game which is meant to maim people?'

We pulled stumps and trudged home in angry silence. Gunther had decided that we would return by a different route, for a reason. We reached a small sports-field, which belonged to his school. There were about sixty small boys, aged perhaps from eight upwards. They were practising the art of throwing dummy hand-grenades (no wonder Hitler's *Wehrmacht* outshone all its enemies in this respect!). We watched.

'Now *that*,' Gunther said triumphantly, 'really has some purpose – not like your English cricket!'

I suppose he was right, in a way.

TERENCE PRITTIE

German cricket clubs also had contacts within the continent. In 1890 the Danes arrived in Berlin and played a very keenly contested game on and off the field! Labouchere et al unearthed this account by Ludvig Sylow, a member of the Danish eleven who made that first foreign trip.

# Denmark v. Berlin

On our arrival in Germany we were met by a Berlin gentleman, Herr Laur . . . we were expecting to meet an all-German side, but when the match began there turned out to be only one German playing, and even he was replaced after the first innings by an Englishman. The spectators were in the main English and American Embassy officials and their wives, but the Prussian Home Secretary, von Gossler, was present, and we were presented to him.

Our opponents had spared no expense. A huge section of Pempelhofer Field had been enclosed especially for the match – the distance from wicket to boundary being 134 yards – and a professional player had been brought over from Breslau (!). The umpire, who was also a professional, was not the least important player on their side, as it turned out.

We batted first and managed to score 70, our Scotsman, Smart, being the only one who did much. When we fielded, our bowlers found they were tossing the ball much higher in the air than usual, and in particular Henrik Buchwald suffered by this. After two overs we examined the ball, and found it had no weight stamp on it. Luckily we had a regulation ball with us and it was agreed that we should use this. We soon found a length but now the professional umpire began to take an active interest in the game. He talked to the batsmen continually, giving them tips on what the bowlers were doing, and we had to speak to him several times about this before we finally managed to silence him. We got them out despite everything for 46.

In our second innings Axel Kalko got his eye in, and the Berlin side soon had all their fielders spread out along the boundary. Unfortunately for them they had made the ground so large that we could not have sent the ball as far as to where their fielders were, however hard we hit it. Fives and sixes all run were quite common.

We made 99 leaving the Berlin side 120 to make, and by seven o'clock they had scored 30 for four wickets, and felt themselves to have a good chance of winning. So did we, and we went to bed early that night.

We got a surprise when we arrived at the ground the next day. Their captain told our skipper, Axel Kalko, that they had purchased silver medals which would be presented to the winners after the match. If we gave him half the value – 40 marks – then we would have a chance of winning them. If not, then the Berlin club would keep the medals themselves. This had not been agreed upon in advance and led to some discussion amongst us; some of our players thought the Berlin club ought to be told they could keep their medals, but in the end we paid the 40 marks, since this would at least enable us to get the match started.

Half an hour later we had them all out for 78.

Their captain, an Australian named P. Dennys, then demanded that we play a return match immediately, in which it was stipulated that our Scotsman, Smart, should not be allowed to play so that we would be all Danish. (The Berlin team consisted of eight Englishmen, an Australian, a Scot and a Dutchman.) We agreed to this, and as a sort of gesture reversed our batting order for this second match.

We still won by 86 runs to 44, and the medals were presented to us by Mr Dennys amidst a deathly silence.

They were inscribed 'The Victorious Eleven', which we thought was very suitable.

P. C. G. LABOUCHERE, T. A. J. PROVIS AND P. S. HARGREAVES,
*The Story of Continental Cricket*

**Even as Hitler's plans were coming to a head some noble attempts were made to develop cricketing contacts. In 1937 the Gentlemen of Worcestershire toured, as was revealed in *Tales from Far Pavilions*, and in 1938, the year of Munich, Somerset Wanderers visited Berlin.**

# Somerset Wanderers in Berlin, 1938

Felix Menzel continued to state in the right quarters that the Germans wished to extend their cricketing contacts, and such statements were featured in August 1938 in such newspapers as *The Times*, the *Daily Telegraph*, the *Daily Express* and the *Daily Mirror* under headings like: AN APPEAL TO MCC or THE GERMANS WANT TO PLAY CRICKET or THE NAZIS SAY HEIL CRICKET.

An association of cricketers from an area comprising Crewkerne, Martock, South Petherton and Yeovil was named 'the Somerset Wanderers'. They reached Berlin via Dover, Ostend and Cologne on Sunday, 31 July, where they were met by Felix Menzel himself.

In his speech of welcome, Menzel appealed to British cricketers to encourage the game on the Continent. His idea was that MCC should organise an international cricket championship, and provide a cup. In one of the earliest known references to something akin to a 'World Cup' competition, Menzel continued: 'The cup would be played for in England by an MCC side, and teams from the Continent such as Germany, Belgium, Holland and Denmark. Of course, the British team would win, but the following year she would have to defend the cup in one of the other countries. This would give a wonderful impetus to cricket on the Continent, and would provide an opportunity of British and Continental cricketers getting to know each other. . . .'

Very generous hospitality was organised by Herr Henner Wolter and Herr Boos and, among other ventures, the tourists visited the largest milk factory in Europe, the first in the world to pasteurise milk on a commercial scale, and several world-famous 'beer-gartens'. Feeling the strain of the tour and the intense heat and facing improved opponents, on 6 August they met a Combined Berlin Eleven at the Reichssportfeld, the venue of the Olympic Games, where their batting fell below previous standards. After the Berliners had made 77, they fought to reach 87 for seven wickets declared and, at the close, the former were 90 for six wickets. It was a draw honourable to both sides. The Berliners had set an orthodox field, and it was very difficult to score runs, especially off Felix Guido Menzel.

A week of good companionship and generous hospitality reached its climax in a Banquet at the Hotel Russicher Hof, at which Herr Breithaupt, chairman of the German Football Association, presided. Another presentation took place, a porcelain statue of a lion mounted on an ebony base. On this festive occasion, Somerset Wanderers responded by singing *We've come up from Zummerzet.* . . .

'Chamberlain and Munich' was only a month or so away, and reminiscences of this tour end on a sad note. While in devastated Berlin very shortly after peace returned, Len Pitcher – a member of the crew of Field-Marshal Montgomery's personal aircraft – attempted to find some of the cricketers he had played against as he had their addresses, but he was unable to trace anyone. All he found was a shop that the Somerset Wanderers had visited; he was recognised by the proprietor's wife – and she advised him to leave for reasons of safety, as he was in the Russian Sector!

JAMES D. COLDHAM, *German Cricket*

During the two World Wars cricket in Germany did not die. In Berlin, league matches were held throughout the host-ilities, 1917 excepted. Similarly in the Second World War Felix Menzel (he had toured in 1930 and played the English touring teams of '37 and '38) kept the game alive by recruiting Dutch and Dan-ish workers and some Indians to play in Berlin between 1940 and 1945.

At the same time a number of 'Tests' were played in German POW camps. Even when cricket gear was not available the game still lived on in these camps.

Terence Prittie is again the reporter.

# Anglo-Australian Quiz

In the summer of 1941 I was moved from 'fortress confine-ment' in Poland to a more 'normal camp' for British and Commonwealth prisoners-of-war in Biberach, a small market-town in the southern province of Württemberg. In fact, the four hundred or so officers confined there saw nothing of Biberach from the moment of arrival to that of departure, for our camp lay just over the top of a steep hill and our view took in green fields and red-roofed villages with, maddeningly, the faint outline on a fine day of 8,000 foot-high Säntis, forty miles south and in Switzerland.

Most of the Commonwealth officers had arrived before the British contingent, and six of us were thrust into a room which already contained a dozen Aussies, big, fit, bronzed men, dowered with bluff good humour and powerful lungs. On the whole the two groups got along well; occasional tiffs almost always sprang from the accusation, or complaint, that all Britons suffered from liver at breakfast-time. As there was nothing to eat for breakfast, we might have had some reason.

We had to keep ourselves amused for long hours, for officer POWs did not have to work for their captors. It was not easy. Then, out of the blue there arrived for me the sort of present that Father Christmas had never had the wit to deliver – *Wisden*, 77th edition, for 1940. I became, instantly, the good friend of at least ten out of the dozen Australians.

I had bought *Wisdens* since the age of twelve, and my Aussie chums found pleasure in questioning me out of this, the only *Wisden* which ever reached a British POW camp (and how on *earth* had the German censors let it through?). But they wanted to take part themselves, and they had an available 'champion'. He was a huge man, about seventeen stone of him, with red hair and blue eyes, and he played cricket for Bendigo, in the State of Victoria. He was nicknamed 'Bluey', oddly because of his red hair and not because of his blue eyes – an Australian quirk.

The idea of an Anglo–Australian quiz was born. 'Bluey' was said to be good, indeed very good, on Australian cricket, but he did not claim to know anything much about what went on in England. So the quiz would deal exclusively with Australians, at home and abroad. Even *Wisden*'s resources are limited; so the quiz would take the form of twice-a-week sessions, after our 'supper' of black bread and acorn coffee, and it would run for four weeks. The question-master, 'Mac' McCormick, was another Victorian. There was to be silence in the room when the quiz took place. Those who were not interested lay on their bunks and read books.

We tossed for 'innings' and Bluey chose to bat first. There were all sorts of questions to be asked – thus, how many centuries had Bradman made, or Woodfull, or Macartney; what Australian had taken 200 wickets on tour in England or had done the 'double' of 1,000 runs and 100 wickets; who was included in 'Largest Aggregates Abroad'; who played for which State; and so on.

Some of my pre-war friends had called me a 'Walking Wisden'; it was my usual bedtime reading and I had a retentive memory. Bluey was a fitter and had worked in a railyard; he had done much less reading in his life than I had. That first quiz set a pattern; I won fairly convincingly, and I batted first thereafter. Mac began to find fresh questions difficult to discover, for there were eight sessions to fill. But he quickly found out that there was a favourite form of question for the audience. This was the year of birth of Australian cricketers.

'When was – William Woodfull – born?' Mac would cry out, seated on an upper bunk, with Bluey and myself on chairs below him. 'Terry Boy?'

I would consider. Woodfull may have played his first Sheffield Shield game in about 1921, but he had been a slow developer. I guessed. '1898.'

Over to Bluey. *Every* question caused terrible mental pain. He would pass a huge paw, the back of it sprouting reddish hairs of great length, over chin, nose, forehead, and back again. Sometimes he clutched nose and chin at the same time. He muttered continuously – 'William Woodfull, did he come to England 1926, or first in 1930?' In anguish, he often swore as well. Then in a tremendous roar: 'Nineteen-owe-three!'

'William Woodfull,' Mac would enunciate slowly, while Bluey gazed wildly at him, 'was born in – eighteen ninety seven! Terry Boy wins again.'

And Bluey would smash a gigantic fist into an open hand, and yell: 'Gawd bugger it! Ee's done it agayn!'

I maintained an unbeaten record, even when the Aussies brought in Les Dixon, who had taken sixteen wickets for Queensland in the 1938–39 Sheffield Shield games, as my adversary. He was imported from another barrack-block in the camp and ran me a little closer than Bluey had. The Anglo–Australian quiz went on, with undiminished enthusiasm, for fifteen weeks in all. Then the camp was broken up, and we moved on elsewhere. I missed my Aussies, and they may have missed me. But I think they missed *Wisden* for 1940 rather more.

TERENCE PRITTIE

The international misunderstanding recorded here can be laid squarely at the
door of British post-war officialdom.

# A Question of Interpretation

In the second week of August I took the Arabs to Germany
to play the British Army of the Rhine. It cannot be recorded that the Army
admin was up to the standard of their hospitality. When we crossed the
Dutch–German border at Benthelm an oriental-looking man in flowing
robes approached and introduced himself as our interpreter. It was
supposed that we were genuine Bedouin Arabs.

E. W. SWANTON, *Sort of a Cricket Person*

In *Tales from Far Pavilions* we failed to
tell any story from William Tell country.
Here, then, is *the* story of Swiss cricket.

# Exploding Balls

The first cricket played in Switzerland might well have been
of a kind which completely overcame the problem of the season-of-the-
year-for-the-game by simply ignoring this factor. Indeed, in England the
same could be said during much of the nineteenth century when cricket-
on-ice was common enough for occasional visitors from warmer parts of
the world to ask if it were a winter sport! The wickets were set in a wooden
block which, upon being hit, would sail right out to the boundary: and if
batsmen found difficulty in braking and turning when completing a run,
such was nothing compared with the lot of the poor bowler who, after
delivery, often found himself arriving at the other end of the pitch before
the ball. Some notable cricket of this type was played at Davos, in East
Switzerland, in the early part of this century (the late Mr H. S. Altham
speaking once of Captain E. G. Wynard, of Hampshire and England,
hitting a stroke here for 20, 'all skated'). In the course of one match within
this category and period a stout lady who was batting had the misfortune to
slip and sit on the ball which, being of rubber, exploded. The fielding side
immediately appealed for lbw, claiming that the ball would have hit the
wicket, but the umpire had other ideas. After declaring that he had never
seen anything of the like of this in his life before, he promptly gave her as
'not out' – in the hope that she might do it again!

P. C. G. LABOUCHERE, T. A. J. PROVIS AND P. S. HARGREAVES,
*The Story of Continental Cricket*

Many Danes and, as we shall see, Helsinki enthusiasts would strongly repudiate the idea that there is anything curious, let alone funny, about cricket being played in Scandinavia. The Danes also seem to suffer from the vagaries of the weather just as much as the English. Yet it takes the bloody-mindedness of an Englishman to continue playing.

## A Diplomatic Incident

It was fitting that an Englishman was at the helm in the game in question, and it added still more weight to the point that he was an Ambassador of Her Majesty, viz Sir Eric Berthoud, who resided in Copenhagen from 1952 to 1956. Shortly before leaving Denmark at the end of his term of office, Sir Eric captained the British Colony side against his old College, Magdalen of Oxford, who were touring Denmark, and some reason existed which made the postponement of this match impossible. As it was, one end of the wicket was under water when play began, and in a downpour of tropical proportions Sir Eric won the toss and elected to take first use of what could be seen of the wicket. Most of the Colony side batted in raincoats, and one of its elder members swore that it took him back to his days in the trenches during the First World War, and began to quote from Rupert Brooke. The Magdalen players in the field, though deferring to the wishes of their distinguished old fellow collegian, had meanwhile begun to grow a bit rebellious, and mutterings were heard when Sir Eric rejected their appeals against the weather in a manner quite out of hand – the umpires being allowed no say in the matter whatever.

It was then that Sir Eric Berthoud showed the qualifications of a man fitted for his high diplomatic office, for in just eleven words he quelled the impending rebellion.

'There will be a champagne supper at the Residence this evening.'

This turned out to be even wetter than the match itself, with the aforementioned elderly player remarking that it reminded him of his first leave to Paris in 1916. But it did not alter the fact that most of the British Colony side were in bed with hot-water bottles at their backs for a full week after the match – and what it cost Britain in exports is better left unsaid.

*Postscriptum:*

When approached a good decade after the episode just described, Sir Eric, from the retirement of his position of President of a village cricket club in Hertfordshire, confirmed that his cricket activities far from ceased after his posting from Copenhagen. Within a very short period of taking up in his next position in Warsaw he had teams playing on the banks of the Vistula – a tiger for the game if ever there was one!

T. A. J. PROVIS

**No game, with the single exception of golf, has been more beset by the problem of missing balls. Peter S. Hargreaves elaborates on the problem with two tales from two widely distant pavilions.**

# 'Why Don't You Fetch the Ball?'
*(translated from the Danish)*

As schoolboys we occasionally had to play on a ground on the hills in Wellington, New Zealand, which had been cut straight out of a slope, with deep gullies on either side. It was rare for any match to finish here, because one could count on losing several balls when they went over the boundary and rolled down into the thick bush at the bottom of the gully.

In 1969 at Silkeborg, in Denmark, I was given the honour one day of captaining my club's first eleven, whilst our junior team was occupied in becoming national champions at Aalborg. During the Silkeborg match, the local young all-rounder, Bjarne Rasmussen, hit a ball out of the ground and into a garden. The local players merely ignored this and quickly obtained another ball so that play could continue.

'Why don't you fetch the ball?' I asked Bjarne.

'Oh – the elderly lady over there keeps them, you know. She's been doing it for years. It's no use talking to her, no matter what you say.'

Silkeborg got a new ground a year after this. Otherwise they would certainly have had to work out some system with their balls.

I didn't think so very much about this episode after this, but a couple of years later when I was in New Zealand I was playing in a Sunday match in something akin to Forty Club cricket for the local branch of the London New Zealand Cricket Club against a team from a private city club from the capital. The game took place on a large ground some distance north of the city in an open area consisting of new housing estates. The bulk of the houses were bungalows with their own back gardens, but with no more than a row of low stakes separating these from the cricket ground. In the back garden the master of the house sat in the sun and read or dozed.

The composition of these teams was nearly always strong, even if most were at the veteran stage. This inevitably led to balls being sooner or later hit out of the ground and into a back garden. Here I recall when it happened the first time. The master of the house rose from his chair, took the ball which he parked down alongside him, and proceeded to relax again in the chair.

'Does he always do that?' we asked one of the players who lived locally.

'Yes, he does, rather. Every time!' he confirmed – and I immediately thought of the elderly lady at Silkeborg.

When the match was about halfway through, the man had gathered up 7 or 8 balls, and I began to think of my schooldays when we played on the ground carved out of the slope. Then a new development came into play. Eight of the players in the city club team were solicitors in everyday life and it was their team which happened to be in the field. From the boundary on the opposite side of the ground we watched them as they came together to discuss the situation which had reached a point of climax, for only a couple of old balls remained among the whole of our combined kits. In the meantime the man in the back garden dozed off again in his chair in indifference.

But the city club team's players were clever. They knew that in such a situation one could always save face, at any rate for the time being, by taking tea, and this they did. I need add here that at least three of these gentlemen were also members of important local bodies and the like. People do not become elected to such positions without owning certain qualifications.

After the tea break the match continued with the remaining balls, but with the express instruction that the bowling be confined to the side of the wicket away from the back garden. On the other hand, it was decided not to restrict the batsmen at all, if they were clever enough to hit the ball right over to the opposite side of the field. In this peculiar fashion the match was completed without any further loss of balls, although right to the last the nerves of all were on edge.

After it was all over I asked one of the city club's players how the whole business stood from the legal viewpoint. He replied thus:

'Oh – that bloke has no right to keep the balls, you see – but neither have we any right to hit them into his private property, unfortunately. . . .'

I became aware of having put a silly question to a man who was soon likely to become a mayor, and for whom considerably more difficult problems were likely to arise in the future. Or would they, I wondered?

PETER S. HARGREAVES

Moving further north and backwards in time we find cricket coming under the scrutiny of officialdom at Riga in Latvia. Perhaps under too close a scrutiny.

# Banned

The authorities had heard that a cricket club had been started, and, evolving from the red-tape-bound consciousness the idea that the game was dangerous, sent a policeman to observe and report.

Now, the policeman was conscientious, and, being desirous to see the game as thoroughly as possible, he insisted on standing among the players. The result was that he joined in it unconsciously – that is, he fielded a ball with his head, and, his skull being rather softer than a swift-flying cricket-ball, he was more or less injured. This convinced the wise authorities that their views as to the dangers of cricket were well founded, and the game was forbidden by order of the municipality.

F. S. ASHLEY-COOPER, *Cricket Highways and Byways*

In a letter to the *Helsinki Cricketer* reproduced in *Tales from Far Pavilions* a Doctor K from Helsinki University criticised the establishment of Helsinki CC in 1974. He claimed he had left England to get away from people who played cricket. Little did he know one of the founders of the club lurked in his own department at the University. The lecturer in question, Silvester Mazzarella, brings us a very entertaining tale involving saunas, smorgasbords and aluminium wickets.

# Cricket in Finland

Although a cricket match of sorts was played in nearby Russian Lapland as early as 1879 (see *Tales from Far Pavilions*), we have no definite record of any cricket in Finland before the 1960s. Indeed, relations between Finland and the cricket-playing world got off to an appalling start. On 19 December 1930 the former England captain J. W. H. T. Douglas, on his way home from one of his regular business trips to

Finland as a timber importer, was drowned when the Finnish ship that was taking him from Helsinki to Hull was rammed and sunk in the Kattegat by another travelling in the opposite direction. The captains of the two ships were brothers and had come too close in the fog while wishing each other a happy Christmas. Rumour has it that an exhibition match was arranged in Helsinki at the time of the 1952 Olympic Games, but we have yet to meet an eyewitness. In the late sixties a Finnish admen's drinking club known as the Kingdom of Palmerston challenged the local British Embassy to a couple of matches which were played on the grass of a large traffic roundabout. Soon after this a mixed bunch of expatriates centered on the British Embassy began making an annual trip to Stockholm, where a cricket club had been founded in the early fifties. It was this group of British and Commonwealth diplomats, businessmen and teachers who decided in 1974 to put cricket in Finland on a more secure basis by founding a cricket club. Some of the diplomats wanted the new club to be known as the British Embassy Cricket Club and controlled by the Embassy, but they were overruled by others of greater vision who held that if the club was to survive it must be run by permanent residents. Helsinki Cricket Club has never had more than about thirty playing members at any one time, but by the end of 1984 it had played 85 matches, winning 37 and losing 33, against sides from Finland, Sweden, England, the Soviet Union and Denmark. More than thirty of these matches have been against Stockholm CC, whom we meet both in Stockholm and Helsinki every summer. We have toured England three times, developing a special relationship with the Scandinavian Bank CC of London and the Vic Lewis CC. Our first match against a Norwegian side has been planned for 1985. The playing season in Finland runs from May to early September and although grass has been tried, matches have usually been played on matting on hard sand pitches, the ground favoured at present – all grounds have to be hired from the city sports authorities – being Kaisaniemi Park, which lies in the centre of Helsinki between the Botanical Gardens, the National Theatre and the railway station. Filmgoers will have seen it in *Gorky Park* – the murders were committed at just about the point where our senior fast bowler Ira Ebanks begins his run-up. The Helsinki XI has included at one time or another natives of Australia, Barbados, Finland, Guyana, India, Ireland, Israel, Jamaica, Pakistan, South Africa, Trinidad and the United Kingdom. After eleven years, five founder members are still active: Sayid Ayub (Pakistani), Ira Ebanks (Jamaican), Francis Looby (Trinidadian), Bjarne 'Fred' Sumelius (Finnish) and Silvester Mazzarella (British of part-Italian descent). The outstanding batsman during this period has been John Cole, an English recruit from football who has learned his cricket almost entirely in Finland, and the outstanding bowler Ira Ebanks.

Looking back, one remembers the usual incidents common to cricket matches anywhere in the world, and much more besides. The ritual of the annual weekend in Stockholm: leaving Helsinki on the ferry at six p.m. on the Friday evening, going below for team sauna and beer as soon as the ship is clear of the harbour; then a rich smorgasbord dinner followed by dancing and drinking till the small hours. Then, for those who are up early enough, the Stockholm archipelago bathed in early-morning May sunlight, brightly painted wooden summer houses and blue-and-yellow flags nestling among the islands' trees. Arrival in Stockholm about nine a.m. and matches on Saturday and Sunday, one of them usually against the recently-formed Stockholm Pakistani CC. On the Saturday evening parties given by our hosts, and one Sunday straight from the ground to the harbour to embark for home at six p.m., arriving exhausted but in time for work on Monday morning after another night of eating, drinking and dancing, most of us not appreciating the spectacular view of Helsinki from the sea (the best way to arrive for any new visitor). Small wonder, perhaps, that Stockholm tend to beat us in Stockholm while we have a better record in Helsinki. Stockholm CC have permanent use of a grass field with a hard mat-covered playing strip in the suburb of Gubbangen (the name means 'Old Man's Meadow' – highly appropriate for some of us). Here over the years many hard battles have been fought on what is always a lively wicket. One year we arrived to find the pavilion (a hut on wheels) the wrong way round, but a group of Swedish firemen playing football nearby obligingly came to the rescue and towed it round with their fire-engine till its door and windows were facing the field of play. On another occasion the local park authorities had forgotten to mow the outfield with the result that scoring had to be mainly in sixes; a cracking drive along the ground would be stopped by the grass before it had gone twenty yards, and when one man had his stumps spreadeagled by a fast ball it took us several minutes to find the bails. I shall never forget the expression on Stockholm wicketkeeper Manu Lund's face when, in another game, he took a ball which had passed between Howard Smith's stumps without touching them.

Memories of Helsinki, too. Matches played in May sunshine hot enough to take off your shirt, but with banks of old snow still unmelted under the trees – ideal for cooling beer, you might think, but any bottle put there would be gone before you could say 'Helsinki Cricket Club'. Or the scorer being distracted by friendly Finnish people asking him to explain the game to them while their small children run off with his pencils (the famous tea-towel description of cricket as being a series of ins and outs has sometimes helped on occasions like this). Once last season it was a case of 'police stopped play'. It was not us they were interested in but two youths mugging a woman across the field beyond the square-leg boundary, and they set off across the middle of the pitch at the double to arrest them. We cheered them on. Tim Moorey, who used to keep wicket for Helsinki in the mid-seventies, remembers the Moscow team of the period (none of them Russian) fielding in Cossack tunics in a bottle-strewn outfield watched by mystified groups of pretty girls while a man from one of the Finnish dailies photographed the batsman at the non-striker's end, rightly judging that that was where most of the action was. Nowadays we do use imported stumps but Francis Looby, who has access to factory tools, has made several attempts to put genuine Finnish cricket stumps on the map. One of our problems being to keep stumps firmly in place in sandy soil, his first model, made of wood, were equipped with murderous-looking steel corkscrews. Unfortunately, when hit they tended to snap in two, the top half whistling dangerously past the wicket-keeper's head while the bottom stayed upright in the ground. Next Francis tried aluminium, producing a magnificent set indistinguishable in shape and colour from the real thing even down to a little logo – except that when you examined it closely you found that, instead of 'Gray-Nicolls' or whatever, it said 'Electricity Keeps You Warm' in Finnish. These stumps were so heavy that several men were needed to carry them on to the field and even Ira couldn't knock them out of the ground. When struck they produced a disconcerting clang and tended to bend and stay bent. Straightening stumps is more than it's fair to expect of an umpire, as one official protested after grovelling on hands and knees with a hammer for several minutes. As I said earlier, we did once try grass, but despite the help of the groundsman of the nearby Helsinki golf course, preparing an adequate wicket and keeping it in condition (and protected from footballers) proved too difficult. One problem was that the grass in Finland takes so long to recover from the winter that you aren't allowed to play games on grass in public parks until mid-June. Another was that the motor roller was kept in a shed half a mile away, and at top speed moved so slowly that it took half an hour to reach the distant corner of the playing fields allotted to us. Someone always had to be deputed to keep it on a lead, so to speak, to ensure that it did not go berserk in its quiet but relentless way and flatten the odd child or animal. And of course it was half an hour back again after the match.

The Helsinki XI is still largely expatriate, though a link to what we hope will be a future generation of native Finnish cricketers exists in such useful players as Fred Sumelius and Esa Saloranta, who both first played cricket in England. Another early Finnish cricketer was Pertti Räsänen, possessed of a remarkable eye. As a batsman, he specialised in fierce pulls which were so effective that it was some time before anyone noticed that he was holding the bat with his hands the wrong way round. On being told he obligingly reversed his grip and square-cut the next ball past point for four.

One of the main problems for a cricket club in Finland is to be taken seriously as a going concern, and with this in mind in 1981 and again in 1984 we produced a magazine, the *Helsinki Cricketer*, intended to entertain and inform. In this connection it was a very important moment for us all when Finland's second cricket club was founded in 1983. Known as the Rest of Finland CC, because its players come from all over the country, it was founded in Kuopio largely on the initiative of Nicholas Smith, English conductor of the City of Kuopio Symphony Orchestra (see Richard Burlingham's story of the Martian who watched cricket in Helsinki).

SILVESTER MAZZARELLA

As Silvester Mazzarella points out, the Kingdom of Palmerston played a number of games against the British Embassy in the late 1960s before Helsinki CC was formed. Here from *Strangers' Gallery* is the full story, related by Palmerston's 'Minister of Information'.

# Tapiola Tests

'The Palmerston Association is the 'Government in Exile' of the Palmerston Islands, a group of atolls quite a bit north-east of New Zealand. We have a King (nice chap, really) and Constitution (simple); our own flag (lost) and newspaper (published twice); and our own way of spending our leisure time inoffensively. Alas, the membership of this gentlemen's club has dwindled. Its ten-year history is more colourful than its current activities, which are disrupted by the hurried pace of life.

Out pitch is covered with snow and as I stand here, the memories flood back to me . . .

The games we played pass before my eyes . . . I remember every game . . . every player . . . every stroke. . . .

And I remember the day we got a run.

It was deep in the winter of 1966 that our beloved Anglophile ruler, Harald I. Beautylock, stated in his regal way:

'Gentlemen, white clothes against a green field make such a good-looking combination that we must start playing cricket at once!'

We downed a goodly draught of our national beverage (Lahti's 'Blue' beer) in honour of this announcement, and mulled over how this game would fit in with the Palmerstonian way of life. After all, sport in all forms was expressly forbidden in the Kingdom of Palmerston.

Perhaps because of this inconsistency, His Majesty's suggestion was approved so quickly that no one had a chance to object. But after all, cricket is not really a sport; it's a way of life. This was pointed out later, to gentlemen of the press who came to witness a little demonstration match. In our opinion, 'other imported British sports such as football are excessively energetic, and golf we considered as a hiking trip gone wrong. But the "lazy charm" of cricket . . . that has a special appeal.'

At any rate, after His Majesty's brief pronouncement, things began moving with amazing speed. By the time the snow and ice of winter had melted and we were basking in the summer of '67, the matter had been taken up officially with some of the British in these parts. To be precise, it was at the summer festivities of the Palmerston Conservative Party in Porvoo. Some of our guests from the British Embassy in Helsinki – Vice-Consuls, Commercial Attachés, and the like – reacted enthusiastically to our enquiries and promised help with training and equipment.

Our first practice was held soon after the summer party . . . on a trotting track in Helsinki! . . . and it was our instructors who came away with most grey hairs. Bowling to us Palmerstonians was a quite new and strange experience. Most of us had thrown snowballs in our time, and some even confessed to playing 'Pesapalo', a Finnish version of American baseball. But now we were asked to contort our arms into knots, straighten them out, and then bemuse the batsman by 'curving the ball in flight', and 'spinning it on the ground'. At the end of this first practice, a sauna, thoughtfully arranged by the Embassy's Vice-Consul, came as a blessed relief for our tortured and twisted limbs, and as an alternative to the pavilion, was an interesting place to discuss the day's play.

Despite our discouraging first contact with cricket we persevered with our training until the end of summer. As well as the technicalities of the game, there were also practical difficulties to contend with, the worst of which was finding a pitch. Helsinki Corporation refused, at first, to believe that cricket had made its way that far north, and then did not consider it could free a single field for our purpose. Help eventually came from the near-by garden city of Tapiola, which kindly allowed us to practice on a patch of grass near a large traffic island. Here, in perhaps the world's northernmost cricket field, a very nervous group of Palmerstonians gathered on 16 September, 1967, for their first match. Our opponents were a group of expatriate British players. Scattered around the field to witness the historic event were over one hundred onlookers – members of the British and American communities and their families, dogs, picnic baskets, and deck chairs . . . and the odd incredulous Finn.

The weather was wonderful, and the match, comprising two innings, lasted five and a half hours, but it was really a no-contest. Palmerston lost 110–60. Sir David Scott-Fox, the then British Ambassador, was gentleman enough to say that he enjoyed the match immensely, but undoubtedly this was more as an entertaining spectacle than as an exhibition of good cricket. However, we Palmerstonians were given plenty of encouragement to continue practising.

Climatic conditions in the summer of '68 rivalled those of a bad English winter, and played havoc with our practices. Even more disappointing was the early arrival of winter, which snowed off a proposed 'Test match' between the Kingdom of Palmerston and Her Britannic Majesty's representatives in Finland. It was not until September 1969 that Palmerstonians again sported their whites on the grass of Tapiola, to take on a British side. But rain stopped play after one innings, and with the scores at 60–31, we conceded our second defeat. Numbed players and a faithful, 100-plus crowd of spectators, warmed themselves in a tea tent, and over steaming mugs of English tea we reflected on failure.

Where had we gone wrong? We had been under expert instruction and had practised for two summers, and yet could not produce much of an opposition to the representatives of cricket's homeland. Maybe we could blame our incorrect dress (mostly doctors' pants and basketball shoes) or our inclement weather conditions (during the 1967 match, one of our ministers questioned H.E., the British Ambassador, about the possibility of purchasing a group of Pacific atolls, which at least would have made warmer practices possible). Perhaps cricket is a game that cannot be learnt in less than a generation; perhaps we were dogs, too old to learn the intricate new tricks of this noble pastime, for all its 'lazy charm'.

Whatever the reason, interest waned in the following summers, and now we play the game no more. Palmerston's short and undistinguished history of cricket is memorable mainly for the spirit of co-operation engendered between the British community and the Kingdom of Palmerston and for the former's enthusiasm to pass on the mysteries of their game. Through this co-operation, born of cricket, we have assimilated other pleasant British pastimes, such as darts, at which we are more adept . . . but that is an elk of a different colour.

KARI KYHERÖINEN (Finland), taken from *Strangers' Gallery*

In 1983 a visiting Martian described his impressions of a match between Helsinki CC and the Rest of Finland CC to Richard Geoffrey Burlingham. Funny lot, the Finns.
The record books of the clubs reveal a 90-run victory for Helsinki.

# Did It Really Happen?

If a Martian had decided to make a landing on the afternoon of Sunday 21 August, 1983 in the vicinity of Helsinki Railway Station and had walked (do Martians walk?) as far as Kaisaniemi, he would have seen a strange sight. Dotted around a green rectangle on the bare earth he would have observed eleven well dressed, athletic young men clad in white trousers and shirts, the latter bearing an inscription which read 'Helsinki Cricket Club'.

He would have known – such is the fame of HCC in Martian circles – that the Club was doing battle. But with whom? He would have seen emerging from a hut bordering the area a succession of human beings, or so he would think, who walked from their hut to the green rectangle in the centre of the arena, and who waved a club to and from while some of the well dressed athletic young men (WDAYM for short) threw an object at them. After a short interval these other human beings would decide that they did not like having things thrown at them and that they should retire to their hut and let others of their kind walk to the green rectangle.

At this point I can reveal that a Little Green Man (or Martian for short) did appear, and accosting what seemed to him to be a native bystander he addressed him.

'Who are these wanderers and why do they walk from their hut at such frequent intervals?'

'Ah!' said the bystander, who spoke fluent Martian as well as Finnish. 'I believe they come from far and wide to do battle with the WDAYM or HCC, and I fear they are coming off second best in the encounter. They are, I believe, called The Rest of Finland and most of them have not waved a club or thrown an object for many years. They are what I am led to understand is called "out of practice!"'.

'Nevertheless,' said the Martian to his bystander friend, 'nevertheless, I was told that their chief also waves a club, if only a small one, in order to obtain the essentials necessary to maintain himself and his family and when he does wave his club the trumpets sound and much music is heard in the land.

'I have also been told,' went on the Martian, 'that some of the chief friends gathered today in Helsinki and who have come from far and wide learned their art many years ago in such far flung parts of the Earth as Australia and England, where for a hundred years or more intensive rivalry has existed for a prize consisting of the mortal remains of ashes of a club.'

'Well, I don't know,' said the bystander. 'That obviously explains why these other human beings, The Rest of Finland, like walking from their hut to the middle and back again so often.'

The two friends continued to watch the contest. They noticed that some of the WDAYM also walked from the hut and concluded that they must be the servants or slaves captured in, perhaps, a previous battle. They observed, too, that those WDAYM waved their clubs and hit the objects thrown at them better than their masters did. They reasoned that because the slaves hit so well there appeared the mystical number 187 upon a board which indicated to them that 'it wasn't such a bad score after all'.

'Thanks to the slaves,' said the bystander.

'Yes, thanks to the slaves,' murmured the Martian. 'But did I not see,' he added, 'another number and was it not 276, and was this not made by HCC?'

'Indeed it was,' said the bystander, 'and are they not a formidable team who strike terror into the hearts of their enemies and whose prowess is known and feared throughout the land?'

'Yes, indeed they are,' replied the Martian. 'Perhaps you would tell their chief that if HCC would like to visit my country some time, we will challenge them to a like contest. In my country we call it cricket and we are known as the MCC.'

RICHARD GEOFFREY BURLINGHAM, *Helsinki Cricketer*

Cricket in Russia remains a shadowy endeavour. The Russians seem to regard the game with suspicion, leaving it to corrupt foreigners to take the field. Allen Synge in *Strangers' Gallery* provided us with a round-up of Russian views. The historical background is supplied by *The Story of Continental Cricket.*

# Soviet Spectators

An appeal to *The Times* produced a number of recorded sightings of that rare bird the Soviet cricket spectator. Maurice Cornforth found an intelligent student in a Dr Georges Samoskin of the Institute of the Academy of Sciences in Moscow, when he accompanied him to a Leicester–Middlesex match. 'If they don't improve their run rate, they don't stand a chance,' the good doctor was already opining at the tea interval. A Russian journalist, again induced to Lord's by Mr Cornforth, was impressed by the calm with which a batsman accepted an lbw decision. 'Doesn't he protest? Doesn't he argue against this decision?' he demanded. The same spectator, applying the principles of Dialectical Materialism, arrived at a profound statement about cricket, 'This game exemplifies on the part of each opposing team the Unity of Offence and Defence.'

Another report of Soviet exposure to cricket finds an embassy official at a loss to understand how the founder of Lord's could have kept a pub. 'Was he perhaps a proletarian lord, like Lord Silkin?' In yet another reported incident, a Slavic visitor to Lord's watches an afternoon's play in total silence and finally announces, 'In Russia we do not have this game.'

According to Mr C. C. Lloyd, a Moscow newspaper recently put its finger on a fundamental problem to understanding: the words 'croquet' and 'cricket' are practically indistinguishable to the Russian ear. Sir Bernard Lovell, however, has an unusual anecdote of Russian readiness to follow the game.

In 1961 the Academy of Science in Moscow requested the co-operation of Jodrell Bank in re-establishing contact with their first Venus space probe, and Dr Khoderev and Professor Alla Massevich, the distinguished lady Soviet astrophysicist, were despatched to assist Sir Bernard.

'When Saturday afternoon came I insisted to the bewilderment of the two Russians that I was the skipper of the local Chelford cricket side, and must leave them to play cricket. But Alla Massevich said that her instructions were to remain with me wherever I went, and insisted on coming to the match. Unfortunately it was an exceedingly wet afternoon and her mystification about the English game was increased by the fact that we spent hours in the pavilion waiting for the downpour to cease. This did not result in much clarification; but subsequently it certainly led to a number of Russian stories about the habits of English astronomers!'

ALLEN SYNGE, *Strangers' Gallery*

## Russian Relations

The natural question of whether Russians have played cricket at all at any time can certainly be answered, but we would first like to draw a little attention to a passage written by that most genial writer and genuine lover of this game, Sir Alan Herbert. Before the outbreak of the Second World War he produced a short account in one of his books of witty essays and impressions, the chapter title of which was the intriguing one of 'Cricket in the Caucasus'. In this he described the harrowing experience of the large and husky Russian who, in the course of a match organised by the State, suddenly found himself obliged to bowl against the sweet and delicate lass of his affections who was among the players of the other side. As a fast-bowler by nature, he was obviously in the horrible dilemma of either endangering his beloved by bowling in his habitual fashion (even if attempting to take her wicket quickly) – or possibly risking all manner of penalties if he attempted to hold back his fire. He decided to flout the authorities at last, and tossed up 'slow ones' to his sweetheart in an effort to preserve her love even at the risk of whatever consequences he would be open to for doing this – altogether a most touching little anecdote!

Much of the information on the earlier history of the game in Russia we again have to thank Mr John Arlott for supplying us with an extract or two from F. S. Ashley-Cooper, the essence of which is as follows:

Although the great land in question has never been associated with cricket, it will surprise many to learn that at least three of its Czars had had some acquaintanceship with the game to various degrees. In 1814, for example, a match played by Eton boys at Frogmore, Windsor, was watched by Alexander I in the company of King George III and Marshal Blücher, and some time later Nicholas I likewise attended a match, played at Chatham Lines. On taking up a ball that had fallen near him, Nicholas was heard to pass the comment to a colonel: 'I don't wonder at the courage of you English when you teach your children to play with cannon-balls.' Nicholas II went much further than either of the others, however, by having a cricket pitch laid in the grounds of the Imperial Palace at Peterhof.

For many years the former Russian capital of St Petersburg possessed at least two clubs – the St Petersburg and the Alexandrovsky – even if the grounds were rough to play on to the point where it was often 'extras' that top-scored. When the first game was played in St Petersburg, moreover, the ground was surrounded by troops – simply because the authorities were far from certain of the nature of the display about to take place. But in time 'Island v. Town' or 'Left v. Right Bank of the Neva' became accepted as annual fixtures, and were often played in intense heat.

But it was when a number of St Petersburg students decided to master the game's intricacies that complications entered this blissful scene, for the party entrusted with translating the laws of play seemed to have experienced difficulty in determining the length of the pitch – which he calculated as being in the vicinity of about twelve feet. Add to this his finding that no fielder could approach within forty feet of the batsmen, and the achievements of the very first match played under the Russian version of the laws were most interesting, to say the least. At this initial attempt one batsman scored what must surely have been every bit the equal of Sir Donald Bradman's reputed century-in-three-overs by notching a hundred runs in ten minutes – simply because he had but to jump out of his crease to score a run. During this impressive performance, on the other hand, his partner was obliged to live decidedly dangerously while being hit all over his person. If he got plenty of the ball, though, paradoxically he got nothing at all of the bowling, simply because here as well the translator had ignored the rules relating to both batsmen running at the same time. Whether this was purely an oversight or because the party in question regarded the point as nothing more than a useless waste of energy, however, we shall probably never know.

Another account worth mentioning from Ashley-Cooper is his description of the reactions of the inhabitants of St Petersburg – as it was then – to a visit by that vessel which seemed to pop up in so many parts of Europe in the latter part of the last century, namely the Prince of Wales's Royal Yacht *Osborne*. Quoting from *Scores and Biographies*, we can reveal the following reference to a match in St Petersburg on the Cadet Corps ground in 1875, which was played between British residents and the crew of the yacht:

'Great astonishment was created in the minds of the natives by the performances of some fifty bluejackets from the Royal Yacht who, with that dauntless gallantry that always characterises the British tar, played rounders with promiscuous cricket-balls throughout the afternoon, varying the game with leap-frog and bull-baiting. A message, indeed, arrived from the "chef de police" demanding an explanation of the presence of this "force of warriors" in the midst of the Russian Woolwich. The answer was apparently satisfactory, as the "warriors" were allowed to depart unmolested, all evidently delighted with their day on shore.'

P. C. G. LABOUCHERE, T. A. J. PROVIS AND P. S. HARGREAVES,
*The Story of Continental Cricket*

Soon after the end of World War II the relationship between East and West fell into stubborn silence. Part of the problem of the Cold War was a failure of communication and understanding. In this, as two letters in *The Times* reveal, cricket played its part.

# Not Cricket

Sir,
    Your correspondent Mr Eason (July 20) is mistaken in thinking his bankers' soft ball affair was the first cricket match to be played in Moscow. On various occasions during the war, the Russians put the Stalin Stadium at the disposal of elevens from the British Mission and Embassy and some stirring if rusty matches ensued on matting wickets with genuine gear. I was detailed off to captain the Mission side and though this afforded me some satisfaction in giving orders to more senior officers it was also a heavy responsibility in view of our sparse but attentive audience of Red Army officers. It was clear from their reaction that our allies despaired of these 'flannelled fools at the wicket' ever putting into effect the long-awaited 'droogoy' front.

Yours faithfully,
ALAN C. JENKINS

Letter to *The Times*, 23 July 1962

Sir,
    Cricketing metaphors are without a doubt perfectly intelligible to English readers who play the game, but are they to the Russians, who do not? What, for example, do they make of the following extract from your leading article on 11 March:
    [Mr Khrushchev] 'feels himself free to lob ideas on Berlin and Germany because he had done most of the bowling since his Note of November 27 and the West – apart from Mr Macmillan's appearance in Moscow – has been stonewalling.'

Yours faithfully,
HAROLD LOCKLEY

Letter to *The Times*, 13 March 1959

**There are people who are trying to forge new links between East and West. A report on the activities of Doug Hudson.**

# Trans-Siberian Cricket

Doug Hudson is the lead singer of Tundra, a group specialising in the folk music of Kent. He has his own record company, Sweet Folk All Recordings Limited.

In the season of 1982 he set out from Rainham Park Station with his Scottish friend, Alex, to bring cricket to the Trans-Siberian Railway.

Hudson was dressed throughout the tour in a club blazer and flannels, Alex in blazer and kilt. They first set up their mobile stumps in Gorky Park, and although they drew only a small crowd the game must be the first ever recorded in this arena.

On the Trans-Siberian Railway they persuaded a growing number of their fellow Russian passengers to play cricket at each station stop.

As the journey progressed many of these Russians were bowling with impeccably straight arms and several had mastered the arts of off and leg spin – and even the googly and the 'chinaman', although this expression was not popular with the Russians.

Hudson is trying to interest Glamorgan in a promising pace bowler called Sergei who took 6 wickets for 10 runs at Severodino.

At the last stop the tourists drew a crowd of 120. Hudson's and Alex's next overseas engagement is a cricket tour of Mount Kilimanjaro. A film company will be following with cameras.

**Our Polish allies were called upon to perform many feats of heroism during the Second World War, such as spearheading the assault on Monte Casino and joining us on those ill-fated operations around Arnhem. We did not know, however, that they were also called upon to play cricket. The following anecdote describes the gallant response.**

# Poles Apart

Air Chief Marshal Sir Christopher Foxley-Norris, looking back to the Battle of Britain, remembers a charming Polish interpretation of cricketing ethics: 'During lulls in the fighting we played desultory scratch games of cricket and our emigré comrades naturally joined us, some showing considerable potential talent. In the Autumn we enjoyed a stand down period and a cricket match was staged, England versus The World (Polish, Czech, French and Canadian pilots). I was the self-appointed England captain, but a deputation from the opposition called on me to protest. Inwardly I was rather hurt but their (Polish) fast bowler explained matters: "Sir, we have trouble with our officers' code. If I bowl you down I shall be disloyal to my commander. If I do not, I betray my comrades. Could you not act as referee?"

ALLEN SYNGE, *Strangers' Gallery*

# Post-war Poles

Sir,
I think I can tell when and where the first cricket match took place in Poland. It was early in the summer of 1946 on a football ground in Warsaw, the two teams being composed of members of the British Embassy staff. The air attaché captained one team and I captained the other. In the eighteenth-century tradition we had a wager of 5,000 zlotys on the match, the rate of exchange between the pound and the zloty being at that time a matter of opinion.

Unfortunately for me, shortly before the match two clerks in the air attaché's office had to be replaced, and both their replacements were more than competent fast-medium bowlers. The air attaché's team won.

One of the difficulties we encountered was that of persuading small boys in Polish, without the advantage of a public address system, why they were welcome to throw the ball in after it had crossed the boundary line and not before.

Yours faithfully,
PATRICK HOWARTH

Letter to *The Times*, 6 September 1975

In Italy, apart from a number of games arranged to keep French and Neapolitan officials busy during the Napoleonic Wars (we wonder at the spectacle they made in the Royal Gardens), it was left to the British Army to play up and play the game.

# Rest and Recreation

During the summer our Regiment enjoyed a month's rest in the toe of Italy. Free from parades, and with little to occupy our time, it was inevitable that someone should eventually suggest forming a cricket team. The position of captain is no sinecure in any team. Yet I fancy that even Mr Selincourt's enterprising Gauvinier would have been fully occupied by the difficulties and barriers with which we were faced. However, a meeting was held, and I was elected captain by vote, or perhaps by 'conspiracy'.

Taking stock, on the credit side I could place a regimental kit, complete apart from wicket-keeping gloves, and a universal keenness among the potential players. On the other hand, we had no ground, and, once that was found, no matting for the actual pitch. The first obstacle was soon overcome. Foraging through the scrub which stretched around the camp, we found a large space of sun-baked earth. An hour's voluntary 'jankers', removing scattered rocks and bushes, and we had our field ready, with mountains on one hand and the Mediterranean sparkling blue on the other.

The coconut matting delayed us rather more. The only length in the regiment adorned the floor of the Officers' Mess, and there, prudence dictated, it must stay. So, for three days we scoured every salvage dump in the area, and eventually, on the verge of despair, we succeeded. Bullying sundry sergeants into a promise to retain the matting for us, we harried our officer until next day we arrived at the dump, complete with signed chit, and bore off the matting in triumph.

Fixtures were easily arranged, and after two hours' pillion-riding I had the names of several local units on our fixture card. Our last difficulty was solved when the Salvation Army Welfare Officer loaned us 'keeper's gloves.

Our first eleven chosen was largely experimental. Only two of our number had played within the last four years, and that game was staged in the Western Desert, with one bat, a tennis-ball and a leg-boundary marked by a minefield. Deep square leg saved many almost certain fours that day!!

We played, and lost our first match amidst considerable amicable barracking, but we learnt a great deal. Noël Coward has written, 'Mad dogs and Englishmen go out in the mid-day sun.' We did for our first game, but later the general rule was play between five and eight, each side to be limited to ninety minutes' batting. We also learnt that the pitch would always be lively and favouring the bowler; again, even a first-class stumper needed a long stop. The only safe way to field in the outfield was to get right behind the ball or be beaten by an unexpected bounce off one of the innumerable bumps.

The day before our next match malaria took a hand. Both our slow bowlers, left-hand off-break and right-hand leg-break, were laid low, and, to fill my cup of sorrow, the wicketkeeper paid the price of eating too many peaches, and went to hospital with dysentery. So, once our opening bowlers were taken off, there was no one to take their place, apart from one man who relied on in-swingers – and in this climate a bowler can bowl till his arm drops off and the ball will not swerve an inch. We lost again. After our batsmen had done well, the bowling was slaughtered to the extent of 170 for 3, a score which, on these pitches, was colossal.

Consequently, our eventual victory was all the sweeter, coming as it did against the area's strongest team, the staff of the local hospital. In their previous twenty games, they had lost but one, and this defeat was practically solely attributable to the all-round capabilities of Watts of Surrey. Their captain claimed their ground as the best south of Naples and I think he had justification. The field was uniformally level, and strange to relate the outfield was grass. Yet the wicket aroused our greatest enthusiasm. Matting laid on concrete, it was fast and true, and for the first time we knew we would drive a half-volley with confidence and lay back to a long-hop. Hitherto on the other pitches, the former were liable to kick head high, and the latter prone to scurry along the ground.

Of the game there is little to say. Our weak bowling must be bolstered by impeccable fielding and good batting, and to this end we practised incessantly. It worked. Never a man put a foot wrong, and, inspired by their support, our fast bowlers worked heroically. Unchanged, in ten overs each on a batsman's wicket, they took five for 30 and five for 36, and the stars were dismissed for 68. An opening stand of 30 put us on the way to victory, and after anxious moments when the fourth, fifth and sixth wickets fell at 65, a hook for four finished the game.

We ended our programme by beating our previous conquerors. Unfortunately we have to be soldiers first and cricketers afterwards, and, with a team at last moulded together, we had to forsake cricket for a less pleasant pastime. But we'll be back, and maybe our next match will be in England.

G. R. HOLLINGWORTH, *The Cricketer Annual, 1944–45*

Lieutenant P. S. White, RA, explains a further complication to playing cricket in
wartime Italy.

# Movement of the Pitch

Out here there are no grass cricket pitches; the actual wicket
consisting of a strip of coconut matting twenty-two yards long and about
five feet wide. Armed with one of these mats and a bag of cricket gear one
can have a game going in a matter of a few minutes on any old flat piece of
desert. This is extremely handy, particularly when on the move. On
several occasions we have played an innings during an evening and then
finished the match on the following evening on the same mat wicket but
perhaps two hundred miles away. Who knows, the day may come when
touring sides will take their own wicket with them and not only toss for
innings but also toss for wicket – ours or theirs – what fun!

LIEUTENANT P. S. WHITE, RA, *The Cricketer Annual, 1944–45*

The Islands in the Med prove safe cricketing havens. Our first visit is to Malta in the
company of one W. J. O'Reilly (not the
Australian spinner), who was garrisoned
there at the turn of the century.

# Eclipse in Malta

The chief matches were played on the Marsa, a tremendous
parade ground, large enough to hold the entire garrison of Malta. Many
games were played at once, and all hits were run out. I remember once
going in to partner Capt H. W. M. Yates, a Hampshire county batsman,
who had then 111 runs to his score. In the next ten balls he scored, and we
ran, 39 runs. Having helped him by running nearly eight hundred yards in
a temperature of over 120 degrees, I was preparing to receive my first ball.
To my disgust, the innings was then declared closed, Captain Yates
having reached 150. I was furious, and came out, bathed in perspiration,
not having had the chance of a solitary hit.

Seeing the name Sfax mentioned in a Middle East communiqué
brought to mind a Regimental Cup tie which was played at Malta during
an eclipse of the sun in 1904, the finest effect of which was to be seen at
Sfax, in Africa. As the sun darkened, the batting side wished to stop play,
but the fielding side insisted on going on, so for about fifteen minutes the
match continued in a weird, artificial sort of candle-light. Fortunately, for

the good of the game, the bowling was erratic, and eventually the batting side proved the winners of the match.

A very remarkable underhand bowler flourished in Malta about that time. One could hardly call him a lob bowler. He whizzed the ball from wicket to wicket all along the ground at a fast pace, starting with an outward swerve, and ending with an inward curve towards the middle and leg stumps. I should mention the pitches were concrete with coconut matting covering. He was most accurate, and the terror of all orthodox batsmen. On one occasion his victims included two ex-Surrey county players in Capt. H. S. Bush and Lieut. Spring, both being clean bowled. To defeat this type of bowling one had to keep the bat glued to the ground. Useless the theory of playing to the pitch of the ball. There wasn't any.

In Malta I batted and was not out for three weeks. The explanation is that at the end of the first day's play in a Cup tie I was 20 not out, and the next day the Governor of Malta ordered sudden manoeuvres which did not terminate till three weeks afterwards, when my innings was continued, ending at 34 runs.

W. J. O'REILLY, *The Cricketer Annual, 1940–44*

**Following on from Malta we have a quartet of pieces reporting the strength of Cricket in Corfu.**
 **Major John Forte delves into the history and terminology of the game. A country vicar gives us his impressions of the island in the nineteenth century. Then, before we allow Henry Blofield to bring us up-to-date, we reproduce a letter to *The Times* questioning the spirit in which the game is played in Corfu.**

# Palla and Balloni

'The 23rd April being St George's Day,' writes Private Wheeler[1] in his letter home dated 2 May 1823, 'His Majesty's birthday was celebrated . . . The Esplanade was the grand rendezvous where all kinds of sports was to take place . . . Various was the games,' he continued in his peculiar English, but strangely no specific mention is made of cricket.

[1] See *Wheeler on Corfu* by John Forte

This is unfortunate, for Wheeler had already in a previous letter mentioned a cricket match being played on Brighton racecourse between his regiment, the 51st, and the 3rd Hussars, on 18 June 1816.

However, Major Harry Ross-Lewin of the 32nd Foot, stationed alongside Wheeler, writing in his memoirs of the same occasion tells us, 'The officers of the garrison played such manly games as fives and cricket.'

The fives court(s) must have disappeared with the Protectorate (1815–1864), but the Esplanade has remained the Corfu Cricket Ground ever since.

It was not until 1835, however, that two Corfiot clubs were first formed, though in the meantime the local spectators and potential players had obviously been coining their own cricket terminology, which has remained the same to this day, viz:

Cricket – play. Pitch – tapetto (Italian rug, mat, carpet). Crease – simadi (mark). Bat – palla (now pronounced balla). Ball – balloni (Italian). Bails – rolinia (Italian). Pads – ghettes (Italian). Gloves – gantia. Abdominal guard – isinto(?). Bowler – bollerr. Batsman – batsman. Wicketkeeper – fermadoros (Italian fermare, to stop). Run(s) – ronia (corruption). Score – scorr. Over – overr. Wide – wide. Guard – messi (middle). Out – sotto (Italian under). Caught – apo psila (from high). LBW – apo podi (from the foot). Long hop – primo salto (Italian first jump). Yorker – pintz (corruption). Leg glide – pissini (back stroke). Full toss – bombada (Italian bomba, bomb). Slips – tsimades (literal). Out – How' dat (Umpire's decision). Cross shot or square drive – traversada (Italian traversare, to cross). Straight drive – issia (straight). Bye – bye. No-ball – no ball. Snick or cut – kofti (chopped). Bump ball – psilittis gis (high from the ground). Block – fermaro (Italian fermare, to stop). Declare – afini palla (to leave the bat). Fielding side – kato (down). Batting side – pano (up). Break – strifto (spinning). Stump – xylo. Bowled – apo xyla.

## Italian Influence

It will be noted that some of the terms are Greek, some Italian, some English, and some a corruption. What is intriguing is that apart from architecture, the only Italian influence which has survived after four hundred years of Venetian rule concerns a game which the Italians have never played.

Rowland Bowen, the well-known cricket authority and historian, points out, however, that in fact the earliest reference to the game in print occurs in the year 1598 when Florio's *World of Words* translates the words 'SGRILLARE' as 'to play cricket and be merry'. Furthermore the Pretender James III was playing the game in Rome in 1718, while a Colonel Maceroni and other nobles were playing cricket at Capodimonte only a year or two before the game was introduced into Corfu.

Nevertheless, the Italian influence can hardly stem from this source, and the obvious explanation must lie in the fact that although it was decreed in 1817 that Greek would become the official language of the

Ionian Islands, nevertheless Italian continued to be the generally accepted 'lingua franca' in most walks of life, among the upper and middle classes.

**Laws in Greek**
With the blessing of the MCC, the Laws of Cricket have now been translated into the Greek language through the offices of the Anglo Corfiot Cricket Association, which was formed at Lord's in 1871 under the presidency of Lord Orr-Ewing and under the sponsorship of *The Cricketer*, who organise the annual Corfu Cricket Festival.

But I, personally, cannot visualise any Corfiot umpire paying even lip-service to this 'new-fangled' innovation, and I somehow suspect that the existing terminology will remain as long as cricket is played on the Esplanade, and that future generations of frustrated batsmen will continue to retrace their dejected steps towards the 'pavilion' having been dismissed Out – 'OW-Dat'.

MAJOR JOHN FORTE, *The Cricketer*, April 1975

# Garden of the Mediterranean

In April, 1895 I was playing cricket in Corfu. 'It is the fairest island that exists,' wrote John Addington Symonds, 'and . . . I wonder how Gladstone had it in his heart to resign this garden of the Mediterranean to the Greeks . . . You live in a perpetual Claude Lorraine picture of the most tranquil beauty.'

Never was truer word written; and no one regretted more the end of the British occupation than the Corfiots themselves.

The one surviving role of the old country, when I was there, was the cricket. It still flourished. There was a men's club; and all the little boys who could procure, or manufacture, a bat and ball played the noble game. In addition they used the English terms, though their language was mainly Greek. 'Innings', 'run', 'catch', 'bowl', 'stump', 'score': one heard the familiar words coming from the lips of dark-skinned urchins who could not speak English at all.

I do not know why I should have taken a cricket-bag to Corfu. Eric and I journeyed thither in February, and our object was to shoot in Albania. But my old bag went with us; and, when our shooting was over, we found 'the Golden Island' so pleasant that we stayed on for another month.

One day an English warship – HMS *Collingwood* – anchored outside Corfu Harbour. Immediately a deputation from the men's club called at our hotel. If they could arrange a cricket match, between the Island and the ship, would I play for Corfu? I said I would.

**Barren Waste**
The fixture was made. The day of the match arrived. I made my way to the

ground. *The ground!* I have played on some bad wickets, but that was the worst! It was on the Great Square, near the citadel – a barren waste, almost destitute of grass. The wickets were pitched on a footpath, since that was considered the smoothest spot. There was no matting – simply the bare earth, worn by the passage of feet into countless little hills and holes and plentifully sprinkled with small stones.

The Corfu captain – an Englishman resident in the island, engaged in business – welcomed me with great stateliness and inquired what position I usually occupied in the field.

I said I would gladly field anywhere he liked, but that I frequently kept wicket.

He announced firmly that he meant to occupy that post himself; without actually saying so, he led me to believe he was extraordinarily good there. 'Do you bowl?' he concluded.

I said I tried to do so.

'What style?' he asked. 'Fast – slow? Roundarm – overarm? – Which?'

I mentioned my humble lobs. I added the information that, on occasion, I also attempted overarm.

He snuffed me out again. He already had a lob-bowler – an excellent one; but would I send down one or two of my overarms for his inspection.

I acquiesced with meekness. He took up his position behind the nearer wicket, and waved me to the further one. 'We shall not do the pitch any harm!' he said.

I felt that was indeed impossible, but I was too tactful to say so. And I felt a certain slight antipathy towards the captain.

I had not bowled a ball for over six months, but my first one happened to be straight, and it hurried along off the sun-baked footpath. It just missed the bails. The captain took it full on the end of his thumb. I regret to record the fact that it dislocated that member.

The captain seemed a little vexed and a good deal hurt. He uttered frequent exclamations of pain and annoyance in three languages – Greek, Italian, and simple English. I pulled the joint in again and expressed my profound sorrow for the occurrence. I also improvised a bandage for his thumb and a sling for his arm.

Then the Naval men arrived – six or seven officers in their eleven – and, after mutual introductions, the unfortunate incident was described in detail. Our own players were also filtering in, and each one was regaled with the same sad story. The captain was most voluble.

The tale appeared to me to grow somewhat with repetition. I caught little scraps of the recital – '. . . pace terrific' – '. . . comes off the ground like lightening', '. . . never more surprised in my life' – '. . . a real fast bowler' – '. . . most alarming!' The sailors seemed to eye me with some apprehension.

The match began. We lost the toss and went out to field, amid the applause of a considerable crowd: Corfu had gathered in force. The captain, who had decided to umpire, but to retain command of his team, threw the ball to me. I felt something was expected of me, and I endeavoured to rise to the occasion. I shared the attack with the lob-bowler (so-called). He was a Greek, with a fine, long, high-sounding name, like Ossopiledonpelion, or Palaeocastrizza, or Polatiano, or Popcatepetl – I believe it began with a P. He played in a bright red shirt and very tight, white trousers. He bowled the fastest 'daisy-cutters' I have ever seen delivered! They zigzagged about on the adamantine, uneven wicket in a manner frankly terrifying. Often they beat batsmen, wicketkeeper and long-stop, and each time that happened it meant two or three byes. My own deliveries sometimes defeated two people, but my scarlet-shirted colleague was long-stopping at that end, and he was almost invincible. His shins must have been made of iron. At the smallest provocation he would hurl the ball at the wicket. I hated that habit of his, for he had a devastating power of throwing, and the wicketkeeper – a poor, craven creature – would always skip out of the way and leave the matter to me. To do the 'terrible Greek' full justice, however, he usually hit the stumps.

We got our opponents out for 40. 'Mr Extras' was easily the top-scorer. Then we amassed 55.

## Tip and Run

But the British Navy was not done with. Time was growing short, so they played 'tip and run'. Often they ran without any 'tip'. Unfortunately Popocateptl's aim deteriorated and overthrows were frequent. They scored 44 for 6 and declared, leaving us twenty minutes in which to make 30. Of course we accepted that challenge and 'went for' the runs. We did it – on the stroke of time – with one wicket to spare.

It was a great match – a Homeric contest – worthy of Greek and Trojan (I mean British) heroes. Though the good ship *Collingwood* finally went under, it was with colours bravely flying. Though Corfu just scrambled home as winners, it was by the most infinitesimal margin. Honours were fairly divided.

I played in two other 'matches', but they were inferior to the first. The *Collingwood* had gone, so there were no genuine opponents. We had to arrange sides – improve a more or less imaginary opposition. Once, I remember, I played against Popocatepetl and I believe he got me given out lbw. I wondered then, and I wonder still, when a ball pitches nine times, how many bounds must be in a straight line between wicket and wicket? All the nine or only one? And, if one, is it the first or the last which counts? It is a question for the MCC!

But I captured many wickets. I maintained my reputation.

For the period of one month I was considered a great bowler. A fast bowler! A dangerous bowler! A Demon Bowler! Another Spofforth!

And all on account of one ball, which the Corfu captain took on the end of his thumb!

'A COUNTRY VICAR', *The Cricketer*, April 1977

## At the 'Simadi' in Corfu

Sir,
As a member of a team visting Corfu in 1934, I can confirm that there were 'jagged stones beneath the matting at strategic points'. But whether on such occasions the stones or the matting are arranged with sinister purpose will never be known with certainty in this country. Very properly, all preparations for the game are completed before the arrival of visitors. There is another uncertainty about cricket in Corfu. The game is played without 'boundaries' and batsmen are expected to run until the ball is returned. Around the perimeter of the ground are a number of tables at which the local beauties gather to enjoy the game and light refreshment. Should a stroke by a visiting batsman send the ball among them, it is at once kicked back on to the field of play. If, on the other hand, it comes from a home bat, it somehow disappears among the draperies, and the visiting fieldsman is left to work out for himself just how far the limits of courtesy may be stretched. Whether such partisan conduct is prompted by the will to win or a greater interest in fieldsmen of the visiting team, I shall never know. I was the wicket-keeper.

Yours faithfully,
Kenneth L. Harkness

Letter to *The Times*, 6 July 1950

## Blofeld v. Byron

Ginger beer and cricket are said in Corfu to be the only two remaining legacies of the fifty years of British rule in the first half of the nineteenth century. The ginger beer is still ginger beer, and while the cricket too is authentic enough, it has acquired various Corfiot twists which make the game there beautifully unique and the most tremendous fun.

Where else would one find a game of 33 overs a side; where else would the umpire call 'no-ball' some seconds after the batsman's stumps have been knocked over; where else do spectators sit in comfortably armed chairs under acacia trees drinking ouzo all the while, and where else are games of cricket finished in moonlight?

The ground is unique too. The cricket is played in the small square which stands in front of the formidable old Greek royal palace and stretches out from the last of the shops in the older part of Corfu town up to the medieval castle which stands sternly by the edge of the sea. The pitch is tarmac covered by coconut matting and the outfield, which has only recently been grassed, is, to say the last, rough as well as extremely small.

The palace stands some way back from the straight boundary at the northern end, and opposite it at the southern end about a hundred yards back from the cricket stands a prim, dark green Victorian bandstand, another legacy of British rule. The rectangle is completed by the ouzo drinkers under the acacia trees and they sit with their backs to a stately colonnade and a row of shops and bars which are almost an exact replica of the Rue de Rivoli in Paris.

## Sun and Bikinis

It was primarily with the object of defeating the three Corfiot cricket clubs that just about half the male members of the party of thirty-six arrived at the Cricketer Taverna, just round the corner from Paleocastritsa in the north-west of the island, on 15 September – things like the sun and bikinis may have been uppermost in the minds of most of the others. With such notables as Bill Edrich and Bob Woolmer and the young Notts wicket-keeper, Bruce French, in the party, cricket and the controversial issues surrounding the game at the moment were never lost to sight for long.

It may by now seem that an article written by a member of the party which appears in *The Cricketer* in order to be read by subscribers to the magazine is the equivalent of a captured writer doing his stuff for a captive audience with the managing director, who was of course our captain, peering severely over all our shoulders to see that we get it right.

I firmly denounce all accusations of bias and prejudice when I say equally firmly that there can be few holidays of this type which fulfil all the requirements so splendidly and looking at it purely on a mercenary basis as value for money, it is surely unsurpassable.

We were allowed a week to get acclimatised and to learn to enjoy and to laugh with the infectious enthusiasm of Nikos, the irrepressible *patron* of the Taverna. Nikos's English does not run to much, but his few resounding phrases soon became a part of our holiday vocabulary.

After a week most of the party had obtained pretty high pass marks in ouzo, wine both red and white, and the almost impossible task of not going to bed before 2.30 in the morning. We had sunbathed on beautiful beaches to which we were taken every morning if we wanted, by the Taverna's caïque and its two splendid boatmen. Sometimes it was an all-day trip with a delicious barbecue lunch.

The swimming was brilliant, the food was good, although it tended to be better at lunch than in the evening; there were cars or motor scooters to be hired, although some of the party had problems trying to keep the latter upright and on the road; there were many intriguing restaurants to visit and any amount of Greek dancing.

## Dutch Victory

This was the time of the annual Corfu Cricket Festival and it came as quite a shock to discover that a week after we landed we actually had to take the field against a Dutch side, De Flamingo's. Apparently their best players had gone home and so we approached this particular 'Supertest' with something approaching confidence. Thanks to a splendid 60 by Richard Umbers, who won a rugger Blue at Cambridge in 1954 and from his form in Corfu must have come close to a cricket Blue as well, *The Cricketer* scored 164 in 33 overs. It might have been enough, but all I need say of our bowling that day was that we lost by nine wickets, and for the Dutchmen, T. Vermeulen made 77 not out, mostly as a result of some remarkable straight-driving.

This was obviously a setback, but the managing director of *The Cricketer* and his splendid wife, with a little bit of help from Bill Edrich, who flatly refused ever to go to bed until he had sung every song which has ever been written since 1933, soon restored our morale. Unhappily the next day happened to be your correspondent's birthday and a marvellous party was arranged. But a combination of a local band, an excellent dinner, wine unlimited and some Greek dancing meant bed at three, which was counter-productive.

Gymnasticos were our opponents the following day. After heavy rain the outfield was extremely wet but Richard Umbers and Bill Edrich playing with great skill took us just past 150. Our two splendid fast bowlers, Charles Madden and David Brocklehurst, then bowled right through the innings and we won by 28 runs. The game ended at one minute to eight, by which time the moon was shining brightly and in the field we were being dazzled by the headlights of passing cars and for the last ninety minutes the light was awful, but it was all part of a typically bizarre Corfiot experience. Most games finish in the dark and there is the story that lighted candles were once fixed to the stumps to show the bowlers what to aim at. If one suggests starting a little earlier than three o'clock those in charge look at one and smile charmingly.

The clocks went forward an hour that night and we planned to start at 1.30 the next day. And we did, approximately. Pheaex, the club which has only just been formed, were our opponents and after Richard Umbers and Mark Streatfield had given us an ideal start the rest of us collapsed and we were out for 119 – we played 30 overs each in this game.

It was now that our captain, who never missed a trick, made his one bad mistake. He insisted that your correspondent should open the bowling and I was told later the plan was to give this new side a few runs at the start. It transpired that the young Corfiots found very slow, rather stiffly-delivered leg-rollers almost unplayable and if I say I took seven for 34 I know that no one will believe me.

We now had two days' rest and recuperation and had two wonderful all-day trips on the caïque in brilliant sunshine. We found that Byron, our last opponents, whom we played the day before we flew home, had recruited three or four of the best players from Gymnasticos and were pretty keen to win. Again Richard Umbers and Mark Streatfield put us off on the right foot and Streatfield went on to reach 78, the highest score of the tour, mostly with a massively powerful square-cut. The rest of us hardly did them justice and Byron needed 149 to win.

They had lost three wickets early, and Yannis, their best batsman, had had to go back to the airport to work. The middle produced a strong recovery and in a thrilling finish which one could hardly see from cover point, let alone from the boundary, because of bad light, we won by seven runs when Yannis, who had made an urgent return from the airport to bat number 8, was brilliantly thrown out by Peter Thompson from short extra-cover with one over left. Incredibly the leg-rollers claimed four more victims, but much the best bowling came from Messrs Madden and D. Brocklehurst.

The cricketers were given tremendous support all through from the female members of the party. They almost always turned up, they clapped like mad, ordered drinks with considerable vigour, they shared the scoring and if one or two were caught shopping at critical moments, one must not be too harsh. I don't think anyone who was there will ever forget these two weeks.

HENRY BLOFELD, *The Cricketer*, December 1977

Our correspondent from Malta also took
the field of play in Crete. W. J. O'Reilly
reports from a narrow ravine.

## Cretan Fables

As I was stationed in Candia, Crete, in 1899, I can assure them that much cricket has been played there, and a left-handed English Test bowler has performed great deeds on the Cretan subsoil, for that was the constitution of the playing pitch. No suitable field being available, the 'ground' was in a long ravine, fairly flat, but a bit gravelly, making fielding a work of art.

The width was about sixty yards, and the length half a mile. After great deliberation, boundaries were fixed as follows: a hit to the wall on either side of the ravine counted two; a hit over the wall, about 150 feet high, scored six. All hits not touching the wall, run out in full. This was a fine inducement for enterprising straight driving, and hits of eight, nine and ten were common. I often wish some of our county stonewallers had graduated on that ground in Crete. The most spectacular hit, however, was a six, which occurred not more than four times in a season.

Looking back now at those sixes, I can say on any county ground they would have resulted in 'caught from a "skier" at square leg'.

Coming back to the name of the Test bowler mentioned above, I wonder if some 'old hands' will recognise him as 'Sailor' Young, who, after leaving us in Crete, went home, played for Essex, and for England in the Test matches in 1899, and in later years was a first-class umpire, with a peculiar habit of gazing into the skies to signify 'not out'. Young wrought havoc on our mud pitch, built up as it was of hard mud, after excavating rock to a depth of two feet. His bowling analyses are not in any official records, but they included items such as: 10 wickets for 3 runs; 9 for 6, and 8 for 0. A little moisture on a mud pitch, and you have the bowler's 'perfect Paradise', as Young used to explain, and demonstrate to us, to our extreme discomfiture.

Our presence in Crete was due to the fact that International troops, comprising British, French, Italian and Russian regiments, were posted on the island to prevent disorder between the Turks, Greeks and Cretans (the Greco–Turkish war having only just ended). The object was achieved, but in different ways.

The British in Candia interested the natives by their cricket and other sports, and so kept their minds off their grievances. The other European troops, at Suda Bay, unintentionally succeeded in quite a novel fashion – they fought amongst themselves. One day there would be riots between the French and Italians, with the Russians acting as peacemakers. Another time it would be Russians and French fighting each other, with the Italians endeavouring to separate them; and so on. Quite a Triangular Tournament, as it were: but highly diverting to the natives, who forgot their own quarrels.

There is a British soldier living today, who owes his life to the fact that cricket was played in Crete. In a drunken fit of depression, he decided this world was not fit place to live in, and took a mad leap over the top of the ravine. His comrades ran to the edge, expecting to see his mangled body 150 feet below. Instead, they heard the most awful language imaginable, coming from an entangled human form, frantically struggling to free himself from the meshes which encircled him – he had jumped on top of the practice nets!

W. J. O'REILLY, *The Cricketer Annual, 1940–44*

One of the pleasant things about this sequel is the discovery of material on new Far Pavilions. In this section on Levant and Arabia (crude schoolboy geography returns to help us on this one) we have stories from the new pavilions at Turkey, Iraq and the Gulf. First, a tale of wartime cricket in Turkey.

# Cricket in Ankara

This addition to the list of descriptions of cricket-in-unusual-places would have been a good deal more interesting without the twin handicaps of strict security regulations and baggage-stealing natives in Egypt. Wartime regulations forbid the publication of many interesting facts, and some brownish and predatory fellow-creature took a fancy to certain notebooks and photographs, with the result that I have had to rely solely upon memory in writing what follows.

Newcomers like myself thought arrogantly that we were doing something pretty original when we agitated two or three years ago for cricket in Turkey. I remember being surprised and pleased by the gentle correction meted out to me by Professor O. R. Baker, head of the English Department in the Language Faculty of Ankara University who arrived in Turkey during the last war and has stayed ever since. I cannot give an assessment of his prowess on the field, for he has now given up playing, but his enthusiasm is obvious. From him I gathered that there was a time when several clubs competed in a championship at Istanbul and that he had the privilege of captaining an otherwise all Moslem XI. Between the wars cricket was also played at Smyrna and Mersin.

All the same it was not until this war brought a flood of new and extra British blood to the Embassy at Ankara that the game made its appearance in the capital. Stumps, bats and balls and sundries were imported from Cairo and a mat was found, suitable for the purpose.

There is, of course, no suitable grass in central Anatolia. Only intensive artificial irrigation measures prevent Ankara from reverting to the state of howling wilderness from which the great Kemal Ataturk transformed it twenty-five years ago. The matting was laid on a football field made of dust, ash and clumps of tough vegetation. The altitude was nearly three thousand feet and the summer temperature well up in the nineties. Sudden dust and thunderstorms tore across the ground, choking, blinding or soaking players and spectators. Though it had its technical disadvantages, the Ankara ground enjoyed one great compensation – its surroundings were magnificent. High above it the citadel of ancient Angora (or Aneyra if you like to go back before the days of Christ) lay flickering in the heat with its massive fortifications encasing a huddle of mosques and primitive dwellings. Away to the south stretched the parks and boulevards of Kemal's fine new town. Nearby was the great football stadium lately erected in tribute to modern Turkey's passion for western sport. Sad to say, your modern Turk's view of cricket is pretty poor.

He wants the excitement and obvious display of speed and skill of football, athletics, boxing and wrestling, at all of which he is formidable. Personally I do not believe that even generations of preaching would ever win him to the gospel of cricket, but actually the British game never had a chance in Ankara, for the Americans – diplomats and interned airmen – played noisy and energetic games of baseball in the next field, which was much more to the liking of the Turks. Our cricket was usually played before a crowd of one solitary native spectator, a peasant who would squat near the boundary, sometimes with his back to the game, smoking and wondering what it was all about. Once or twice he tried retrieving the ball, but, when we explained that this was *yasak* (the local equivalent of *verboten*) he at once refrained: the Turks are a law-abiding race. Occasionally a booted and spurred policeman would stroll our way to make sure it was no lethal weapon that the batsman brandished and no hand-grenade that the bowler hurled, but he was quickly satisfied and went back to control the crowd which was watching the baseball.

And so it was for our own amusement and for that of a sprinkling of British wives and children that we played. The players would be from the Air or Military Attachés' offices, from the Economic and Supply Missions or from the British Council. Sometimes we would have a Derby between two departments, but more often the sides were mixtures, for we didn't mind why we swiped, chased, and perspired as long as we did so. Most people had either white shirts or white trousers, a few both. As far as I know we only ran to two pairs of proper cricket boots, but one came on the feet of R. J. Parkhouse and travelled in a bag full of miracles of private and personal equipment which had been with him to play in first-class matches at home during his Glamorgan days. Alas for us, he worked in a town far from Ankara and spent his leave on the immaculate turf at Gezira, so he only played one game in Ankara. That one appearance, we felt, however, gave us a good bit of tone.

The heat is sweltering. The dust lies everywhere. The match is timed for 14.30 hours. At 14.00 a lorry with a beaming Turkish *karass* in charge appears at the Embassy club. It is very necessary, for the ground is two miles from where most of us live, there is, of course, no petrol for private cars, the taxis have all gone to the races and the buses are always hideously crowded and often lousy in the literal sense. Gear is packed aboard, then glasses and a lot of bottles of Turkish beer, which, though splendid straight off the ice, is already beginning to feel the heat, and then players. A great many of them are comatose having only just got up (it is Sunday and Saturday night goes on till break of day in Ankara), but the two sturdy sons of the PT expert are full of bounce and enthusiasm, recalling details

69

of last week's game and wondering who will be out first ball on this occasion. A Maltese stalwart of great enthusiasm and greater incompetence climbs aboard. He is wearing an outsize, floppy panama which will inevitably fall off every time he tries to field the ball. The lorry starts with a shattering jolt, as do all lorries driven by Turkish *karasses*, and we sail down the main boulevard past statues, blocks of flats and fine government buildings, swing left along by the Youth Park with its great stretch of water studded with little boats, and finally go in through the back entrance of the stadium to our lonely cricket ground.

The game itself needs no detailed description. Scores are low (100 all out is a lot). Fast bowlers cannot manage more than three six-ball overs, and some not so many. A large proportion of the runs come in sixes, for the boundaries are short. The Maltese stops the ball with his feet and is enveloped in a cloud of dust; a tall young man with bright red hair and a brother who has kept wicket for Essex plays forward with grace and charm to his second ball which never leaves the ground and bowls him neck and crop; a doctor with a fierce military moustache fields talkatively and with remarkable energy; a professor of Pedagogy, badly out of practice after ten years in Japan and wearing spectacles which deprive him of all vision of the ball during the last four or five yards of its trajectory, celebrates his fiftieth birthday by carrying his bat through the innings; a soccer blue makes a mountainous score of 30 by polished violence; an ex-heavyweight champion of a Guards regiment beats the air without effect; the crowd barracks the captain of the British Council side who is altogether too overwhelmed by the beer and the heat to be able to run at all! Strange raucous cries come distantly from the baseball ground; the peasant picks his teeth; the policeman smiles indulgently at the characteristic display of lunacy; storks glide aimlessly overhead, and ancient Angora, which has seen Alexander and Pompey, Byzantine and Ottoman conquerors and other queer strangers, reflects that these are surely the oddest of the lot.

It doesn't matter in the least who wins. Once in a dust-storm the score-book blew away altogether, but we played on. All that matters is that for a time we are each of us back on some field at home. I am sure that each of us stretches his imagination with violence enough to be transported from the middle of the Anatolian desert to Chalfont, Corsham, Ottery St Mary, Blackpool, Wallsend, Nottingham or wherever he would like to be. In war the isolation of belligerents in a neutral country is astonishingly complete, but for an hour or two we can forget it over a game of cricket.

The only other place where I played cricket in Turkey was at Karabuk, the extraordinary steel factory, plumped down in a desolate mountain fastness near the Black Sea. I went to stay with the British engineers who work there and we had a game with a burst ball and a chair leg. It was three in the morning and the pitch lay inside the billiard room of the British club. We broke some electric light bulbs and a window, and the patients in the hospital next door had a disturbed night. But, being true Turks, they were far too courteous and hospitable to complain.

A. W. NEWSOM, *The Cricketer Spring Annual, 1945*

Now a splendid but, alas, anonymous
piece on I Zingari's tour of Turkey in 1923
following civil unrest.

# I Zingari in Turkey

It is interesting to note that amidst all the ups and downs in Turkey, amidst wars and rumours of wars and Lausanne Conferences, an I Zingari team captained by the Commander in Chief, Lietenant-General Sir Charles Harrington, has played a series of enjoyable cricket matches.

In spite of the great history of I Zingari, it is quite certain that the famous club has never before displayed its colours on the cricket grounds of Turkey.

The series of matches was concluded on 19 August by a brilliant win within four minutes of time over a strong team representing the Dardanelles area. The match was played at Chanak before a large number of spectators.

No one would have imagined a year ago, the very time when Chanak was the danger spot of the world, that I Zingari would be playing a two-day match on that very ground, with perfect surroundings, accompanied by the band and pipers of the KOSB and the band of the Royal Sussex Regiment.

The colours of I Zingari are black, red and gold and stand for 'Out of Darkness through Fire into Light'. These words are truly applicable to Turkey and especially to Chanak. Have we not emerged into the light! The light of peace has at last dawned after a long period of darkness and danger. May the light of peace remain in Turkey for many a long day.

The British forces in Turkey, comprising, as they do, battalions of the Grenadier, Coldstream and Irish Guards and the Rifle Brigade, contain many members of I Zingari and it was a happy idea to play this series of matches, the scores of which are given below, the matches played being:

    v HMS *Iron Duke*, won by 264 runs
    v Royal Navy, won by 81 runs
    v The Army, lost by 17 runs
    v Constantinople CC, won by eight wickets
    v Dardanelles Area, won by 93 runs

These I Zingari matches have formed quite a feature in the daily life of the British forces. They have been played in the splendid spirit of I Zingari cricket and in keeping with the I Zingari motto, 'Keep your promise, keep your temper, keep your wicket up', which has, through many difficult situations during the past few years in Turkey, been the orders which the British troops, who are now leaving Turkey, have so loyally carried out.

*The Cricketer Annual, 1923–24*

In Israel they seem to specialise in playing
in unusual places. A report from the practice nets on Mount Carmel.

# 'Mind Out for the Yekke'

When I met my Englishman for the first time it was not a
Romeo and Juliet affair – in fact we quarrelled in public! I was out of work,
on my way to a job interview. In Haifa we do things a little different to
other Mountain towns – we put our cable-car INSIDE the mountain, and
call it the CARMEL GET. (After Mt. Carmel, whose interiors it tracks
through.) Anyway, I emerged blinking into the late autumn sunlight, and
saw a friend sitting with another man at one of the café tables by the
Carmel exit. Thinking to persuade him gently into buying me a coffee, I
sat down. 'Shalom' – I greeted him – 'and who is your friend?' Introductions were made, coffee was called for. Taking a sip, I stared at the
stranger's filthy, blackened hands, and in my poshest type British accent
(copied from the BBC) I asked, 'And what do you do for a living?'
(*Importance of Being Ernest* – Oscar Wilde – much in the style of Lady
what's-er-name saying A HANDBAG!) The next moment I was splutter-
ing inelegantly into my coffee as a ripe Lancastrian retort rolled robustly
round the cafe: 'I work, which is ******* well more than you do.'
Gathering my scattered dignity round me, I made a hasty retreat.

What, I hear you mutter, has this to do with cricket? – patience, dear
readers.

It was a wet night before your Christmas, and I was flat hunting. My
cousin passed me the paper and I spotted one – just down the road. I
decided to pop down before supper. It was dark and wet, and instead of
modern flats it was the German-built houses, of which more later. I
banged on the first door along the row, feeling hungry, depressed,
expecting the worst. Rain dripped down my face, the door flew open. 'Eh,
lass, tha art all wet – coom in Luv.' I had last heard those deep Lancastrian
tones in less auspicious circumstances aforementioned. Taking a deep
breath I entered, and tripped on something round, shiny red, that rolled
into a corner with a dull thud. Barking my shin on something hard, I
walked in. The smell! It was pungent, nose-wrinkling. I was too polite to
ask what it was (later I learned it was linseed oil). I was given a cup of real
English tea (no milk – he'd forgotten it). Then he took me next door, to the
lady who was letting the room.

Over the next few months I worked, and took pity on this helpless
Mancunian. I went in and cleaned his flat one day – buying all the cleaning
stuff, clean sheets, pillowcases (I burned the old sheets; there weren't any
pillowcases at all – just pillows). When he walked in – no pleasure – just
'MY GOD – HAVE YOU TOUCHED MY CRICKET THINGS?
YOU HAVEN'T WASHED THEM OR ANYTHING, HAVE YOU?
. . . STUPID. . . .'

The rolling Lancastrian tones petered out as he stared at his bat, his ball, neatly cleaned, polished lovingly . . . with furniture polish. His flannels clean, washed – and starched. I slunk away sorrowfully.

The next day he came in the evening with flowers, and an invite to dinner – if I'd cook it. Later that evening I was washing up when he called me. Towel in hand I went in and sat down. Clasping me round my pinny, he gazed at me and said, 'Would you follow me to the end of the earth?' I frowned, puzzled, and said yes – then light dawned. 'Are you proposing to me?' I asked. He was. Little did I know I was marrying cricket too (*Tales From Far Pavilions*).

Even if the proposal wasn't romantic, the wedding was – it was out of doors under the stars. Sorry, readers, no arch of cricket bats. Oddly enough, not much of cricket except in one or two speeches and jokes.

I knew that at weekends he'd just disappear – I was at the family, either in Tel Aviv, or Jerusalem. One or two times I would go to see a cricket match – very pleasant.

But now I discovered the reason for the twilight grunts, clunks, crashes and swiping noises that I'd been hearing on my return from honeymooning in Jerusalem. I was told to 'Pick oop bat loov, coom outside.' 'Good,' he said. 'I've got someone to bowl too, and practice batting with – that tree were getting reet battered – Oh, and mind out for the Yekke.' (A Yekke is slang for a German person who wears a jacket or Yekket even in the searing heat of an Israeli summer.) Thus I found myself fending off such strange sounding throws ('You doan't throw! Tha bowls!) as Googlys, Yorkers, etc., or vainly trying to bowl at a bat ('Call that bowling – it's anaemic . . .').

I think I'd best explain that, set at right angles from the road were three long sets of cottages – in the first cottage of the second row lived a doctor who'd converted two flats into a house. Then came us, with the Yekke above, then an American couple with my ex-landlady above. More people lived further down. Flagged paths led down between the cottages – grass lawns separated them, and all was planted with shady pine trees. A path led behind the cottages, and it separated one back wall from the garden of the cottage next door in the third row. It was on this back path that all the cricket practice took place.

My first practice was cooled off by a sudden drench of lukewarm soapy water – descending by way of the back upstairs window from the mop bucket of the irate Yekke's wife. My Englishman said I was lucky – early in the morning it usually was something else, less pleasant.

So if you wonder how English cricketers on top of mountains, in a city surrounding, practise cricket – it is with great difficulty, my friends! Hazards such as pine trees growing in the wrong place, irate neighbours and the odd cricket ball being hit for six and landing with a nasty tinkly crash into the doctor's consulting-room are to be treated with tact and great caution.

YEHUDIT LIPMAN

After practising in confined places, players in Israel then take delight in finding the nearest desert or mountain to play on. Simon Holt brings us the state of play.

# In the Wilderness

In the deep valley at the foot of Mount Sinai, just a few hundred yards from St Katherine's Monastery, the fabled home of the 'Burning Bush', lies the ground of the MSCC. The Mount Sinai Cricket Club is an unusual amalgam of Israeli soldiers, little urchin boys and visiting members of the Commonwealth. To my knowledge they have only played one fixture.

Such was the circumstances of the game that it could be argued that everything wasn't cricket. No willow hit red leather, no flannelled warriors strove in the bright desert light, indeed no one wore white, yet the spirit of our beloved game was there.

We had been woken at three in the morning to stumble up the crumbling track that led us to where Moses had received the Ten Commandments. As the dawn broke over the rocky desert the game was arranged. Thankfully we managed to scramble down the mountain without losing any of our players to sprained ankles and pulled muscles.

A strip was needed among this barren land. Rocks and stones were cleared from a likely spot, two boxes were established as the wickets, a piece of plastic piping became the bat. Some suggested we used the plentiful supplies of Jaffa oranges as a ball. But a few practice shots left us with a soggy bat and batsman and lots of small Arab boys screaming as they ran in pursuit of the bleeding oranges. It was also pointed out that should out citrus break up in flight and some of the segments go to ground and others be caught by fielders, would the batsman be out? No Intercontinental phone was available to consult HQ, anyway no one knew the number of Lord's or Dickie Bird.

Thankfully a rubber projectile was provided by our driver. There was no problem that it was green, it was the only thing that was. Two teams were picked, Australasia v MSCC. On the stone strip every ball that pitched got up rather high. Hooking, pulling and ducking were the order of the day. The wicketkeepers armed with a pair of gloves made their efforts but were constantly having to retrieve the ball from a nearby ravine. The preponderance of small stones around the crease meant that even the slow bowler could get the projectile to turn. One of our Israeli guides was persuaded to play. Placing his M16 rifle on one of the wickets he proceeded to bowl an over of very accomplished leg breaks. Basically because he aimed for a pothole half-way down the wicket.

The batsmen were not totally at the mercy of wicket and bowler. There was a certain satisfaction in tonking the ball so it rebounded down the mountain side, even more when it got lodged up there and the boundary fielders (the furthest of whom was at square leg, it was a very small ground) had to go and get it. Meanwhile the batsmen would keep on running. There was an unfortunate incident when one of the Australasian batsmen was hit by the returning ball, he ended up in the bottom of the small ravine which was just behind the keeper. Luckily there was some thick gorge bushes at the bottom which prevented permanent injury.

Fielding was no one's joy. Diving was out of the question. Once the ball pitched it took off at the most acute angles.

No score remains of the game, that was not the exercise. There had been a sense of joy walking up to the small stone church at the top of the mount to see a new day born. The day had been completed by an attempt to bring the Game to this desolate area. A fair swop, I would say.

SIMON HOLT

**Here is a short report from Iraq. Alas, things may have become a little hotter for cricket in this part of the world since Alec Waugh's visit.**

## Some Notes from Iraq

There is plenty of cricket of the good London Club variety in Baghdad. The local side, the Casuals, which has just celebrated its twenty-first anniversary, has a pleasant ground of its own – an oval surrounded by oleanders. There is no grass, of course, and we play on matting stretched over a surface of specially prepared baked mud and the ball can be made to turn on it quite a bit. We play two-day matches from quarter-past-four till half-past-six, and in spite of the heat – 115 degrees to 125 degrees – a number of centuries are scored each year. The light, however, becomes very difficult in the last half-hour and there is often a collapse when the opening bowlers come on for their second spell, rested during the cool of the day. A side that has 140 on the board for two wickets at six o'clock is by no means certain to get the 160 which it has been set to win. We had a number of exciting finishes last year.

ALEC WAUGH, *The Cricketer Spring Annual, 1945*

One of our well-travelled players describes his adventures in the Gulf.

# Petrol Can Island

The tiny island of Masirah lies off the coast of Arabia and the Sultanate of Oman. It is comprised of rock, sand and salt – barren, without a vestige of greenery – but, in my time, vital as a military communications and re-fuelling station. Almost all of the so-called buildings were constructed from rough wooden and metal frames clad with flattened four-gallon Shell petrol cans – hence its RAF name of 'Petrol Can Island'. The RAF signals and defence detachment there described this tiny outpost of Empire in rather more colourful terms – but, in spite of the incredible heat and much hardship, they played cricket whenever conditions allowed. I went to the the island first at the end of 1943, escorting a six-man welfare and entertainments party in an obsolescent Wellington bomber – the aircraft having been converted to carry a mini-piano in the bomb bay and about a ton of sports and canteen equipment!

The cricket was unbelievably competitive, the pitch impossible, although (on this occasion) the equipment apart from the stumps was in good condition. A relatively new ball became a stringy wreck and then disintegrated within an hour of play, and games were stopped frequently by minor injuries and cries of 'lost ball'. The composition of the home team changed almost on an hourly basis, as players joined and left matches in strict accordance with their radio and radar 'watches' – very confusing for the visiting side – and, to this day, I am convinced that one red-haired airman from Keighley in Yorkshire managed to bat three times in a single innings by adopting the thinnest of disguises! Thankfully, the Masirah team fielded only eleven men.

CHRISTOPHER BOX-GRAINGER, taken from *A Walk to the Wicket*

Believe it or not, the first Test match was *not* England v. Australia, but a stern contest between those two unlikely cricket sparring partners, the United States and Canada. H. G. Robinson sets a much overlooked series in its intriguing context.

# America v. Canada: the Roaring Forties

At a time when sport is increasingly a 'political football' (O jarring term!), the idea of it as a bridge-builder between nations is rather discredited. Yet the first international contest involved two countries – America and Canada – recently involved in border disputes and with a history of enmity over more than thirty years: the sport was cricket.

The origins and early years of this fixture, begun in 1844, lacked nothing in incident and character, as noted in John I. Marder's excellent book, *The International Series*; likewise the preceding history of the two countries. Indeed, a contemporary novelist of the John Buchan type might have been tempted to relate the two. I shall simply recount the more striking items from both and leave the reader to construct his or her connecting skein.

From the mid-thirties onwards, Canada's troubled progress towards self-government inflamed its border disputes with America. Of the five Governors-General in the period, Francis Head was mistaken for his more gifted cousin, Sir Edmund Head; in like fashion, Lord Harris once approved the selection of A. W. Carr, a young Notts batsmen, with the words 'Rather old, but Kent – we can't go wrong there', believing him to be D. W. Carr, a leg-spinner of about fifty. The younger Carr shone, but not the lesser Head, whose four successors all died prematurely, one in a riding accident, the others from disease. One might almost suspect a 'dirty tricks' department among the English-speaking business community, who saw appeasement of the French Canadians in every move towards 'responsible government'.

The blueprint for the latter, E. G. Wakefield's *Letter From Sydney*, was written while its author was imprisoned there – untouched by the early stirrings of Australian cricket – for abducting an heiress. As the Earl of Durham, 'Radical Jack' Lambton, began putting his ideas into practice in 1838, Canada was suffering raids from American-based rebels: one Nelson proclaimed himself 'President' of a government in exile until his followers were dispersed after marching on Napierville, Quebec; W. L. Mackenzie, the John Wilkes of Ontario, set up a Republican Government of Upper Canada on an island in the Niagara River until loyalist 'commandos' from the Canadian side sunk his supply ship, killing an American in the process.

What with the above businessmen favouring union with America as insurance against the French menace and New Brunswick lumbermen kidnapping an American senator, bat and ball chose an odd time to link the two countries. Inter-club contact came first, to a background of baffling intrigue. A man claiming to be G. A. Phillpotts of the Toronto CC turned up in New York in 1840, proposing that the St George's Club travel to play them in Toronto with a return match in New York, the host club to pay all travelling expenses. (The early national teams centred on these two clubs.) The St George's secretary wrote to another Toronto player – named by 'Phillpotts' – to confirm, but significantly the man was away and never received the letter.

When the Americans arrived, they were completely unexpected: Toronto were in fact about to leave for a match with Guelph. Much embarrassed, the Canadians cancelled Guelph to play their visitors and quickly found the culprit, though he was never 'officially' identified. Fishier and fishier. What can have been the motive? A forlorn attempt to sow discord and keep Canada British? If so, it failed handsomely, for this was the catalyst for the International Series.

The great match began on 24 September 1844, in circumstances typical of English cricket's freewheeling days before the age of Grace. A side bet of \$1,000 was involved, the spectators betting a further \$100,000; due to start at 10.00 a.m., the match began at 11.40 before five thousand people. Canada's first innings 82 was the highest total of the match, the odds shifting to five to four on a Canadian victory during the Americans' reply, and they duly won by 23 runs. Twenty minutes later George Wheatcroft, an American player, arrived at the ground for the first time – and this a two-day game! His team-mates demanded he should be allowed to bat, but got the answer they deserved. Where *had* he been? Is it too fanciful to concoct a meeting between Wheatcroft and a secret Canadian delegation, the germ of the 1846 treaty which extended the 49th parallel border to the western seaboard? Certainly, his selection for the next three games against Canada – not to mention umpiring in 1856 – is on the face of it extraordinary: the loosest wandering side would have looked at him askance.

Toronto's Winckworth is the Midwinter of the series: having emigrated to Detroit after the first three games, he played for America in the 1846 fixture. Again, the opportunity for diplomatic sleight-of-hand was there. A Chinaman with one thumb would enhance any tale of intrigue; apart from his nationality, G. A. Barber ('The Father of Canadian Cricket') filled the bill, but did nothing more sinister than improve sportsmanship and bat steadily despite his handicap. The diminutive H. J. Maddock's black beaver hat and deadly slow lobs offer more scope for mystery, perhaps. Fortifying them with his renowned 'chops with tomato sauce' was French, the Toronto professional-cum-cook-caretaker-grounds-man. Heaviside, who played in 1845, is the biggest enigma: Mr Marder thinks it may have been an alias, a common contemporary device – getting time off work is a recurring cricketer's problem. . . . In 1846 the Americans countered with a Mr Rouse, whose top hat, tight trousers and roundarm bowling were all slightly controversial.

They also had a Gatting figure in John Symes, who looked the part but averaged 4.00 in six innings – perhaps a tour of India would have improved his record. The St George's groundsman, Sam Wright, played eight times, both his sons also reaching the national side; the creation of an early Manhattan baseball diamond is, however, a blot on his escutcheon. All these characters pale before cricket's first international incident, a sort of Snow–Gavaskar in reverse, or *The Batsman Strikes Back*. Another Sam, Philadelphia's Dudson, was awaiting a steepling return catch in the fourth game (1846) when the striker, Helliwell of Toronto, charged him to the ground. The Laws of 1702 did in fact allow either batsman – within limits – to hinder the bowler in this way, but Helliwell's free interpretation ended the fixture for seven years. Dudson hurled the ball at him and when the Canadians, despite the bowler's apology, refused to continue, America claimed the match.

And so cricketing discord went hand in hand with national rapprochement: it is all very confusing. Happily, the Series continued almost unbroken from the resumption to 1912 and was revived by Mr Marder in 1963, since when Asian and West Indian immigrants have sustained it.

H. G. ROBINSON

The rude health of the game in North America at this time encouraged a number of teams to tour the two emergent 'Test' countries. In 1859 a tour of English professionals, captained by Frederick Lillywhite, was organised to take on teams of Twenty-two from Canada and the USA. It was to end in the snowy wastes of upper New York State with cries of 'Shiver my timbers, I'm out!' Twenty years later, not to be outdone, a team of Irish tourists set out to test the warmth of American cricket hospitality.

# 'Some Innocents Abroad'

Embark with me on one more tour. The year is 1879, the same year that saw Richard Daft's excursion. The players were not English, but Irish of the Irish, and their exploits are boisterously celebrated in a rare volume entitled *The Irish Cricketers in the United States*

*1879* by *One of Them*. Even more minutely than Fred Lillywhite's book, this deals with the personal adventures of the players, giving less and less attention to what happened on the actual field of play. There is a fascination in the opening sentence: 'There was something unusual going on at the Kingsbridge Terminus, as the American Mail lay beside the platform, awaiting its weekly burden. Here and there might be seen pieces of luggage marked with a strange device. On each was a large circular badge with letters printed in green upon it, which, on closer inspection, were seen to spell "The All Ireland Eleven" . . .'

Who could resist a start like that? The book is a short one of a hundred pages and has thirty-five chapters, all with exciting headings, the first ten of them devoted to the voyage out. Of the visitors, at least four were Hones, all ancestors in some degree of Patrick Hone, author of the recent delightful volume, *Cricket in Ireland*. ('We had a N. Hone, a G. Hone, two W. Hones, and later on a J. Hone, but unfortunately not a single O'HONE amongst the lot.') It is difficult to assess their absolute value as cricketers, but one of the happy Hones at least had something in common with W. G. Grace. He took his bride across the sea with him and the tour was their honeymoon.

What struck the visitors most on landing at New York was the impression they gained that all the men were thin and wore long mustachios and all the horses were thin and wore long tails. It seems an odd phenomenon to be the first that observant in-comers noticed, but then, of course, the New York skyline as we prostrate ourselves before it to-day was not there to be admired in 1879. Furthermore, their first fine careless impression was modified by a second impression that there were also men with short mustachios or no mustachios at all. There were even some fat horses with short tails. The visitors, therefore, seem to have been extremely fair-minded in their observation.

They first took the field in a game against an eleven of the St George's Club. It had been expected that they would play against odds, but the Irish captain made up his mind that, whatever happened afterwards, they must not be beaten at the first attempt. He therefore, despite the protests of some of his men that they would willingly have played against twenty, insisted on equal numbers. As things turned out, he need not have worried. The Irishmen rattled up nearly two hundred and, as for their opponents' reply, 'their first innings closed for twenty-five; their second showed an improvement of ten runs'.

In this cheerful spirit the tour proceeded, encouraged by victories over their opponents by day and relaxed by bouts of banqueting in the evening. The narrative is not crippled by statistics and there is no serious attempt, as in Fred Lillywhite's book, to set down the scores. On the other hand, there is hardly a drink, much less a meal, that goes unrecorded. Even in 1879 American hospitality was overpowering and the author quotes a bill of fare which covers a full closely-printed page of the book and runs the full gamut of culinary ingenuity, from oysters, shrimps and Kennebec salmon, by way of beef, veal, lamb and grouse, to a huge ice pyramid on which the figures of cricketers, lions and eagles were carved, apparently roaming the slopes as though these were their native habitat. In the course of such a dinner, says the author, the pangs of hunger almost ceased to wound. Mark that down for your collection of happy understatements.

The Irish won their match at Syracuse by an innings on a pitch which had once been an old Indian war-path and was full of arrow-heads and flints. It would be a pitiful example of meiosis to admit that this wicket helped the Irish bowlers; the Syracuse batsmen merely heaved successive sighs of relief when their wickets were scattered and they could return once more to the safety of the pavilion. At Staten Island the tourists met a fiercer foe, Ephraim Lockwood's old friends, the mosquitoes. All the Irishmen were attacked, and only one, Mr Casey, secured immunity, mainly because his beard faced the attackers with something like a barbed-wire entanglement. The home eighteen staved off the innings defeat by one run and, in forcing the Irish to bat again to knock off the single, were cheered by their supporters as if they had won a famous victory. The match at Hoboken was won by a 200-run margin, but victory was delayed and only obtained on the stroke of time. So – splendid achievement – 'we saved the match from a draw'.

It was at Philadelphia that the Irish met their Waterloo. In the City of Brotherly Love they had some brotherly cricket, for there they met a team containing as many Newhalls as they themselves contained Hones. There were George, Robert and Charles and the last of these added to the sharpness of his attack by his sinister passion for lemons. One of these he would keep behind the wicket and 'drew inspiration from it for each ball and each stroke'. The defeat of the visitors by this gang of Newhalls was complete and resounding. As each Irish wicket fell a carrier pigeon was sent flying from the score-box to the newspaper office in town, spreading the glad news of Philadelphia's triumphant progress. Ireland's sporting behaviour in the face of defeat received high praise in the local Press. 'Had they been victors they could not have displayed sunnier tempers or watched the fall of wickets with a gentler manner.' But the author of the book comments *sotto voce*: 'The correspondent apparently did not accompany us to the hotel, or spend the evening with us.'

To the return match, played by special arrangement the following day, there was a palpitating finish. Ireland were set 109 to win and when they had reached 107 for nine, the umpire looked at his watch and lifted off the bails. The match was over and drawn. Instantly there was a roar of disapproval from the crowd: 'Go on! Finish!' was the cry. The shouting went on until the two captains, if only to avoid bloodshed, went out on to the field and agreed to start again. The citizenry, in all brotherly love, were determined not to be baulked of a finish and the Irish knocked off the runs in one stroke amid scenes of the wildest excitement. Casey, who had made the winning hit, probably off his beard, was carried shoulder-high into the pavilion, in peril of his life. The finish, however, was nothing to the inevitable banquet, which did not break up until dawn the next day. As the author so beautifully observes, 'all did not leave at the same moment'. The dinner was superb and the decorations were carved in artistic compliment to Ireland. 'There was a melting Hibernia in ice and a harp of the same substance that wept silent tears . . .' The chairman begged that speech-makers would be merciful, but his plea went unheeded. Everybody but one man made speeches. Everybody but one man replied to everybody else. The man who did not make a speech was the one for whom the tour was a honeymoon. Towards the end of the evening, that is, about 4.30 a.m., he was called on to respond to the toast, 'the lady of the party'. The rest was silence.

He was sleeping peacefully.

A. A. THOMSON, *Odd Men In*

**The welcome and the spectacular scenery impressed Richard Daft of Notts and All-England who captained another nineteenth-century tour of North America; but not his Yorkshire team-mates, according to this brief anecdote.**

# 'I'd Sooner Be at Sheffield!'

We had a great treat in seeing the far-famed Falls of Niagara, at which place we spent the Sunday.

I was greatly surprised to overheard a conversation between Pinder and Lockwood on this occasion. We were taking our first look at the Great Fall, at the sight of which most of us were almost awestruck with admiration. The two Yorkshiremen were standing a little apart from the rest of us and Pinder asked Lockwood 'what he thought on't?' Ephraim replied: 'Nowt at all. If this be Falls of Niagara, I'd sooner be at Sheffield!' These two worthies always chummed together wherever we went.

RICHARD DAFT, *Kings of Cricket*

A recurrent bugbear of these North
American tours was the weather. Inevitably they seemed to have been fixed,
perhaps by some crazed Anglophobe
administrator, for late October and
November, and equally inevitably wickets
and players suffered. Here is W.G. himself describing a match at Boston which
was far from being a tea party.

# Dark Hunt for Grace

Our captain, Fitzgerald, was not in the best of health, and
having some business in Boston he entrusted the captaincy to me. When
we got to the baseball ground, on which the match was played, we found it
in a very deplorable condition, heavy rain having been falling all through
the night. The wicket itself was not very bad, but where short slip, point
and mid-off had to stand there was a perfect quagmire. Some idea of the
condition of the turf may be judged from the fact that between twenty and
thirty bags of sawdust had to be bestowed upon the ground before it was fit
for the match. Notwithstanding this precaution some of the fieldsmen
stood ankle deep in sawdust and slush. Our opponents were twenty-two of
Boston, and we got nineteen of them out for 26 runs, when Linder put
quite a different complexion on the innings. He hit up well, and carried
out his bat for 17, the total reaching 51 before the last wicket fell. We
began our innings disastrously, and when Fitzgerald arrived on the scene,
thinking that perhaps only a few wickets had fallen, he was astounded to
find that eight of our men were out for 39. Out of this meagre total I had
made exactly two-thirds, having twice hit the ball out of the ground, for
each of which I was only allowed four, although they were honestly worth
six. Eventually we were all dismissed for 51 – a tie. In went the Bostonians
for their second innings, but Appleby and I dismissed the twenty-two for
43 runs in the course of an hour and a half's play. The one incident of the
innings was a splendid hit out of the ground by Wright, the baseball player
who, being a native of Boston, was one of our opponents. It was getting
late, and darkness would soon be upon us, but everybody was anxious that
we should go in again. We only wanted 44, so it was decided that we
should finish the match if possible.
The wicket was getting worse and worse, the fieldsmen were sinking
deeper and deeper in the mud, and the light was fading rapidly. Our start
was again disastrous. Two wickets went down for 7, four wickets for 8, five
wickets for 11 (by this time it was almost dark), six for 19, and then we
appealed to the umpire for leave to abandon the match on the ground of
darkness. The umpires decided against us, and Fitzgerald went in. A few
minutes afterwards a full pitched ball hit him on the toe – he declared it
might just as well have hit him in the face for all he could see of it – and the

umpire then decided that it really was too dark to go on. Time was called, and in the darkness and damp we concluded the last match of our tour in the West. As a tie in our first innings was followed by our making half our opponent's score for the loss of half our wickets, we agreed that the 'honours were easy'. The match was altogether a very curious struggle, and I have often thought it was very lucky that darkness did come on, otherwise I am sure that we should have been beaten.

After the match George Wright presented each of the English twelve with a baseball. I have mine still, and preserve it as an interesting relic of the wind-up to a memorable tour.

W. G. GRACE, *Cricketing Reminiscences and Personal Recollections*

**What went wrong with England's 1899 American tour? Certainly the cricketing authorities of New York appear to have aroused the ire of the normally benign Prince Ranjitsinhji, as we can surmise from this stern letter to *The Times*.**

# Prince Ranji is not Amused

Sir,

A statement appeared in one of your columns today that the Metropolitan Cricket League of New York met to consider the charge of discourtesy against myself and other members of the visiting team.

From the second paragraph of the statement I gather that the accusations are that myself and other members absented ourselves from the match, and that we played substitutes the next day.

I am naturally much astonished at this most extraordinary statement, and this is the first intimation I receive in any shape or form of this conduct on the part of myself and the other members. After the first day, as is well known, of the first match against Philadelphia I was laid up with bronchitis so that I was not able to take any further part even in that match. But, feeling slightly better, I left for New York and, not a little against my doctor's wishes, to play against eighteen of New York, in which match our conduct is impugned as discourteous. As the travelling brought on fever, I was advised to abandon the idea of playing in the match and to put up in New York, instead of Staten Island with the rest of the team. I was unable to leave the hotel the whole time I was in New York on that occasion.

I entrusted Mr MacLaren with the control of the team as before. The next day the team, as invited by Sir Thomas Lipton, went and saw the yacht race. I trust that my absence did not lead Sir Thomas Lipton to think that I was discourteous to him, as it evidently did the associated clubs of New York.

The next day the match commenced and all our players took part. In the evening Mr MacLaren telephoned to me that he was suffering from rheumatism and would I mind if he had some medical treatment for it in New York, and that both he and Mr Priestley were coming to see how I was getting on. I was naturally alarmed with Mr MacLaren's condition, and replied, 'Come this evening and stop here.' Both of them came and stopped in New York that night. Next day he had some electric treatment. A wire was sent by Mr MacLaren in the morning to Mr Stoddart to take charge of the team in his absence to the hotel at Staten Island, informing him of the cause of his absence and that he required Mr Priestley's assistance; the latter also that afternoon had to arrange for our berths for the passage back, as we were not to return to New York again till just before our departure for home. The wire was not forwarded by the Staten Island hotel authorities on to the ground, and consequently Mr Stoddart was unable to declare innings till lunch time, having waited for Mr MacLaren. The delay in declaring undoubtedly saved the New Yorkers from defeat. Whether Mr Stoddart asked for two substitutes to field or not I am unable to say, as no mention was made to myself by either my own side or by any of the New York authorities. These, then, are the facts of the case. How they can be construed as acts of discourtesy by our opponents I fail to see.

I am cabling today to the Metropolitan Cricket League of New York, the existence of which I only knew through your columns today, for explanation of the matter, and asking them to inform me why I was kept ignorant of their complaint against myself and my team during our stay in America.

I request you to put this rather lengthy explanation in your columns in justice and fair play to the men who did me the honour of accompany me out there, to myself, and for the sake of English cricket, which we represented out there. I take this opportunity of acknowledging our indebtedness to the Philadelphian clubs and the Canadian clubs for their lavish hospitality and kind attention during six weeks of our most pleasant stay among them.

Thanking you in anticipation.

Yours faithfully,
RANJITSINHJI

Letter to *The Times*, 3 November 1899

Snow, mud and occasional frictions apart, the continent of North America was once one of the healthiest bastions of the game. Sadly, as David Gower reports, it now relies on expats and Hollywood razz-mattazz.

# Down in Pasadena with Gower

Come the end of the season, it is happily the fashion nowadays to spend a couple of weeks winding down overseas in warmer climes, under the pretext of playing a nominal number of games of cricket. Add to that the name of a suitable beneficiary and as many supporters as possible and in no time you will be flying west.

Previously we had been to Barbados and Antigua for Vanburn Holder and Barry Dudleston respectively, but this year we decided to go a little further, and under the banner 'California Goes Cricket', we landed in Los Angeles, all supposedly for Norman Gifford's benefit, but as usual as much for our own pleasure and the opportunity to explore new territory, new restaurants and the odd new brew.

Actually, there were a few odd brews, such as Michelob, Coors and Schlitz, to add to the already familiar Heineken and Budweiser. Duncan Fearnley provided the bats (it's OK – I took my own GN100!), Everton Travel organised the tour, and World Airways kept us guessing all the way across the Atlantic.

Los Angeles doesn't quite have the cricketing history or tropical scenery of Barbados, which explains why so often members of our group had to explain our noble game to the ignorant natives of California. Yet those who did understand why we run straight and not out to first base are not short of enthusiasm. And they need it. The two Woodley Park cricket fields that all sixteen local clubs have to share in LA are owned by the city, which is responsible for maintenance. Those responsible actually had the decency to cut the outfield and pick up the grass, apparently in our honour. The clubs themselves do their best to maintain the turf wickets. They have to leave a thick layer of spongy grass on the pitches, otherwise they have a nasty tendency to disintegrate fairly rapidly. Thus even the gentle medium-pacer can extract enough life to awaken all but the most Schlitz-sodden batsman.

A certain tone was set for the fortnight on the first morning with a welcome champagne brunch. Our host guaranteed us sun for the next fourteen days, even though it took some time to break through the smog of the morning. Ted Hemsley stayed long enough to make sure that none of the champagne was wasted before following the rest of us to the poolside. Rumour had it that LA had not seen rain in September in twenty-eight years. That must now be twenty-nine.

Our schedule included two matches against the Southern Californian

Cricket Association, and the big day: a double-wicket competition, with male and female stars of Hollywood, which it was hoped would lure the thousands to the Pasadena Rose Bowl and initiate them into our noble art, thus, I suppose, encouraging them to throw away their baseball bats so that one day we can play England v. USA in front of 100,000 in California, perhaps finding a space in Disneyland!

The two 'proper' games were both suitably relaxed once we had established that none of the opposition bowlers was likely to rival Michael Holding in pace; even then, the splice and bat handle were used more than once in defence.

The opposition, comprising folk of English, South African (quiet), Asian, West Indian and even American descent, would mainly be of good club standard, with one or two capable of playing county 2nd XI. Indeed, one, Neil Lashkari, spent some time with us at Leicester in 1980, having been discovered on a previous visit by Jack Birkenshaw.

For highlights, David 'Let it go, Reg' Steele featured on occasion, enquiring politely from gully: 'Can I have that one?' for a skyer which would have won the first match but instead landed very adjacent to mid-off. (Bad luck, Reg.) And then, during the second game, as the recipient of a singing telegram organised in celebration of his fortieth birthday by thoughtful Jim Cumbes.

The most important cricket, if the least seriously played, came with the day at the Rose Bowl. Not even Ian Botham partnering the Incredible Hulk, nor Geoff Miller with Christopher Lee, could attract the hordes of spectators hoped for – and needed to fill the stadium, with its capacity of 102,000. There was a certain disappointment discernible among the directors of Everton Travel, whose baby this was.

### White Knickerbockers

However, after a tentative start about four p.m., the competition started to warm up. Dressing-room facilities were spacious (American football teams number about fifty in all!), equipped with English beer on some sort of tap, and, in keeping with laid-back California, a mixing of the sexes, though our female 'starlettes' all came ready-changed in their white knickerbockers and 'California Goes Cricket' shirts.

The sun dimmed, the floodlights glared, the temperature dropped, and our girls sought refuge in the massive Press-box, sited at the top of the 92 rows of seats more than 150 yards from the centre of the action, but also full of food and wine to refresh any ailing spectators.

Lou Ferrigno (the Incredible Hulk) borrowed Goochie's 'box' and autographed it before returning it, while the starlettes concentrated on preserving their fingernails if the ball approached – though mostly it disappeared many a mile over the short square boundaries, into the empty spaces on one side or in among the crowd on the other. Even the stars, experiencing cricket for the first time, managed the odd fearsome blow, even allowing for very gentle bowling. My partner, Rick Anderson, caused one fielder to retire clutching his stomach. All this immortalised by the two film crews that also occupied the field, often at very close quarters.

Eventually, Botham and the Hulk succumbed in the semi-finals to Graham Gooch and Tristan Rogers, Australian-born star and heart-throb of *General Hospital* – and, judging by the screams, also responsible for the presence of half the paying crowd.

In the other semi-final Gower and Anderson just defeated Gifford and Patrick Wayne (son of John), despite no-balls and some very sloggable full tosses apparently designed to help them into the final.

So at about 9.30 p.m. the first 'California Goes Cricket' final came to an end, and my partner and I came second. For the stars their first taste of cricket seemed to enthral them. As we celebrated next evening with cocktails with the British Consul-General they all seemed keen to repeat the experience if the chance arose.

DAVID GOWER, *Wisden Cricket Monthly*

**A re-run of All England v. All America was played when the Jack Frost XI toured California in 1975. There appears to have been a mischievous element in the party.**

# Keystone Maladies

The Jack Frost XI cricket club is composed of players who aim to extend the season at both ends. We play on Christmas Day in Surrey and on New Year's Day in the New Forest. We would play on Hogmanay Night in Siberia if anyone cared to ask us.

California cared to ask us for a pre-season tour in 1975. Thirty-three of us left Gatwick on a snowy Maunday Thursday and arrived sixteen hours later in glorious cricket weather at Los Angeles. Travelling as baggage man was one Ian Waller, perhaps our most prolific batsman. Unfortunately Ian had broken his arm on a Swiss ski slope. We were to pay dearly for this mishap, as the reader will learn.

In surroundings as genial as only the Sunshine State can make it, we were introduced to the leading lights of Californian cricket. There was hardly a native born American among them: but we made the acquaintance of the distinguished Savern family, two strapping sons of a father, Dr Clifford Savern, (then in his eighties) who years earlier had claimed the distinguished record of being the oldest man ever to have played at Lord's. Clifford Savern's legendary bowling was not to trouble us during this tour, but we were to be seriously disconcerted in our final game to see the good Doctor, a dietary consultant to many famous American athletes, doing handstands on the boundary. We were also introduced to the Barbadian Donald Weeks (no relation, if you pressed him, to Everton) who boasted a citation from President Nixon which glowingly described him as 'The greatest all-round athlete in the United States'! He was certainly to prove a hard man to dislodge, as was Nal Lascari, an Indian Test cricketer of the 1950s, or at least pressing Polly Umigrar for a place.

Our first match, however, was to be against the full might of British Columbia on the Sir C. Aubrey Smith ground. As good luck would have it, we won. Or was the simple fact that BC's two leading fast bowlers had on the previous evening been rehearsing their run-ups with two of the most seductive starlets it was to be my privilege to see in Hollywood, albeit from a distance?

It was now that Ian Waller began in various ways to demonstrate his frustration at being a mere one-handed baggage man.

His first warning signal was an announcement, mysteriously posted in our hotel, advertising 'Lobster Dinners only $2!' The minor riot this caused in the hotel foyer was intensified the following evening when a second announcement appeared apologising for the disappointment caused by promising genuine lobster dinners at only $1.50 for that night.

It was necessary to be on our best behaviour when we were entertained by the British Vice-Consul. We were discreetly reminded we were the first English cricket team to visit the official residence for thirteen years – the previous visitors having been Yorkshire in one of their more self-destructive moods. Ian thanked the Vice-Consul effusively for the lavish hospitality we had received, but he added darkly, 'As a personal friend of the Foreign Secretary [then James Callaghan] I will be obliged to inform him that you are wasting an extraordinary amount of tax-payers' money on a bunch of cricketers!'

We moved hastily to our final fixture, which was a full scale 'Test' between England and America. With a first innings total of nine wickets for 75, it seemed to me that a fearsome responsibility rested on my shoulders. As I adjusted the last buckle of my pads I was conscious that the honour not only of Jack Frost but of all England rested on my meagre batting talents. It was at this point that I was unnerved by the spectacle of two police cars hurtling on to the pitch with sirens screaming 'Mr Gill', and a bulky patrolman menacingly accosted me: 'We have orders from the State Governor that you are to ring your Prime Minister immediately!' No prizes for guessing who was responsible for this Keystone comedy!

Perhaps the most poignant comment on our tour came from a batting star of the Dodgers. We found him, on returning late one evening from a hard day in the field trying to save the England v. US Test, asleep in the hotel lounge with a cask of Watneys bitter between his knees (the gift of a kindly sponsor). 'Hey, you guys,' he complained on waking, 'I was told to present this to you at 10.30. How long does it take you to play a game of cricket, for Heaven's sake!'

TONY GILL

'Overpaid, over-sexed and over here!' was
the sour witticism repeated around English pubs, at least those that had any beer,
regarding the friendly wartime invasion of
the American ally. But here, without over-
extending themselves, we find the GIs
putting up a modestly convincing performance at cricket. What was England
complaining about?

# Yank Overs, Over Here

Cricket history was made on Saturday, 18 September, when
two all-American teams played a match 'Somewhere in England'. The
sides were composed of USAAF officers, representing Station No. 'X'
and Station No. 'Y'. Having won the toss, Station No. 'X' put the
opposition in, a traditional custom in Saturday afternoon cricket, and
Captains Mitchell and Podwajsky opened the innings to the bowling of
Captains Johnson and Barry. Both the batting and bowling were much
above the standard that the English onlookers had expected, and Captain
Mitchell, with a sure eye and a strong forearm, was particularly impressive. Thirty-one runs were scored before the first wicket fell, and when
Major Hartman was clean bowled by Lieutenant Hagel, the score was 56
for 2. From this point, to the end of the innings, Captain Mitchell
completely dominated the attack, which however never became ragged,
and Captain Barry deserves a special word of praise for his bowling. His
final analysis was seven for 56, and it would have been still better, if
Captain Mitchell had not been dropped in the deep when he had scored
32. Profiting by this mistake, Captain Mitchell went from strength to
strength, and it was a delight to watch the fielding side applaud when he
reached his fifty. However, he had little support from the later batsmen,
and he was finally last out, having scored 60 out of 92, a stalwart
accomplishment for one so young in cricket experience.

Ninety-two was a formidable total for Station 'X' to face, and they fared
disastrously against the bowling of Captain Podwajsky, who bowled
unchanged for a final analysis of five for 13. Only Lieutenant Taylor, who
opened the innings, played with any confidence, and although Captain
Johnson hit two fine boundaries, the whole side was out for 35, and the
match was over.

The fielding and throwing of both sides was good, as was to be
expected, and Captain La Croix gave an excellent display of wicketkeeping. The bowling was above expectations, and the fact that no fewer
than nine batsmen were bowled bears testimony of its accuracy.

When the game was over, twenty-two enthusiastic American officers
discussed the afternoon's play, and the possibility of a return match was

foremost in everybody's mind. This may or may not materialise, but in any case, the match has whetted the American appetite, while those of us Britishers who were fortunate enough to be there will never forget the spectacle of our American friends playing keenly and enthusiastically, and thoroughly enjoying an afternoon that had been devoted to England's National Game.

MAJOR E. R. T. HOLMES, *The Cricketer Annual, 1940–44*

**Recently we had the opportunity of seeing the 1932–33 MCC tour of Australia replayed on our television sets. 'Leg theory' was seen to stifle the great Donald Bradman's talent. Yet had the damage not already been done in Canada and America?**

## Sidelight on Bodyline

In 1932 Bradman, who was never seen in New Zealand or in South Africa, or in the West Indies, took part, with several other leading Australian players, in a long and exhaustive tour of both countries led by Arthur Mailey: and it was Bradman who established the Canadian individual record. It was the last tour in North America by an Australian side which could have been ranked first-class if it had played any matches against first-class opposition: as it was, it scythed down such opposition as it encountered, losing, inevitably, the odd game in such a long tour. It could well have been this long and tiring tour which to some extent exhausted Bradman when it came to the famous 1932–33 tour of Australia by Jardine's men.

ROWLAND BOWEN, *Cricket: a History of its Growth and Development throughout the World*

Despite W.G., despite Donald Bradman, despite the brave efforts of wartime GIs to familiarise themselves with the national game of 'My British Buddy', cricket fixtures between England and the United States have become a lamentable rarity in this century. It is therefore a pleasure to record one happy landing for a trans-Atlantic cricket buff.

# Wicketkeeping in Mowtown

It made a change from making the usual fearful hash of trying to land at Harvard.

It was May 1955, and the flying training took place at the Royal Canadian Air Force base at Centralia, near London, Ontario. A hotch-potch of we RAF, RCAF, Belgians, French, Turks, Portuguese, Norwegians and others from NATO countries were all trying to learn to fly; this was Canada's contribution to NATO – organised chaos was the watchword.

At the weekends, however, more traditional pursuits became the order of the day. The RAF contingents at Centralia were a happy hunting ground for the recruitment of cricketers for the local clubs, including the Canadian National Railway Cricket Club at London. I played a few games for them at places like Hamilton, Windsor and Stratford-on-Avon, and one weekend in late May found myself on the way to Detroit, selected to play for South Western Ontario against the State of Michigan. Our captain, who worked for the CNR, was a high-class West Indian player called Jimmy Cameron and I believe he played a few times for the West Indies before the war. The game took place on a lovely warm Saturday on Belle Isle, which is in the middle of the Detroit waterways.

The State of Michigan turned out to be Michigan CC and consisted of ten West Indians and one Maltese, who kept wicket. They all attended Michigan University. There was a definite carnival atmosphere about the whole affair as the British Consul opened the proceedings by bowling the first ball.

There are three abiding recollections of the game. One, the Consul's first ball was a wide – I was keeping wicket! Two, SW Ontario won, largely through the efforts of the said J. Cameron. Three, I was arrested by the Detroit Vice Squad that evening – for drinking (beer) under age (I was 19 at the time) in a delightful West Indian night club. Fortunately the British Consul was still with the party and a quiet diplomatic word was sufficient for my release. It was Coke for the rest of the night!

JEREMY WARD

If you think we have been somewhat pat-
ronising about American cricket during
the course of this section, you will savour
the inevitable come-uppance. Tony Greig
(in his pre-Packer heyday) with a world
All-Star team in tow invades the Shea
Stadium with every expectation of a
Beatles-like triumph. As with all good
tales there's a sharp sting in this one.

## Damn Yankees Hit Cricket for Six

Now I know that the sun has finally set on the British
Empire. The Yanks have licked us at cricket.

We have long learned to live with American supremacy on the tennis
court, in the boxing ring, on the golf course and running track.

But twenty-eight years after the US knocked the full England soccer
side out of the World Cup we consoled ourselves that there was always
cricket. They couldn't beat us at that, we said.

Having watched our three best tennis players, Buster Mottram, John
Lloyd and Mark Cox, fail to survive the first week of the US Open, I took a
short walk across the railway tracks from Flushing Meadow to the
towering Shea Stadium, sure in the knowledge that the Yanks would be
shown a thing or two when it came to a real game.

But it didn't work out that way. The American All-Stars beat an
international side of former Test cricketers by seven wickets.

The world All-Stars were all out for 124 in thirty-three overs. The
legendary Sir Gary Sobers made just three. And when he bowled he was
hooked and driven to the boundary.

Former Australian skipper Greg Chappell scored a single and Tony
Greig was top scorer with 18.

Yet Sobers and Co had the help of erstwhile England wicketkeeper
Alan Knott and fast bowlers John Snow and Andy Roberts. Not to
mention South African opener Barry Richards, and such masters as West
Indian Roy Fredericks, Australian David Hookes and India's Sunil
Gavaskar.

To be fair, the conditions were slightly different from those at Lord's.
The pitch was a matting strip laid across a baseball diamond used by the
New York Mets.

And every ball was accompanied by a commentary in language which
would hardly be understood in the Long Room at Lord's.

The American team were drawn from the New York area, which has
seventy clubs whose players are, in the main, of Caribbean descent. But
their hero was a New Zealander, Dr John Millener, who took four wickets
for 13 runs in seven overs.

Grieg, who is accustomed to putting a brave face on disaster, told me afterwards: 'I am disappointed at our performance – and surprised at theirs. We made the mistake of not coming here earlier. It is out of season for most of our team and we were not prepared. And most of us haven't played on a matting wicket since we were ten.'

Burt Smith, the president of Cricket Classics Inc., who put on the match, kept telling everyone, 'This is my great American dream.'

But for eleven cricketers and a handful of Brits it was a daylight nightmare.

The only mercy is there's a newspaper strike in town. With luck, not too many people will get to hear about it.

LAURIE PIGNON, *Daily Mail,* 4 September 1978

We've all met them. Flannels pressed, kit bag bulging with accessories and offering to sell us a six-month-old bat that 'isn't quite the weight' they wanted. Richard Gordon tracked down one of this species deep in the Brazilian jungle.

# Theoretical Cricket 1,000 Miles into the Brazilian Selvas

I am a purely theoretical cricketer, my combination of ineptitude and enthusiasm more painful for onlookers than for myself. I resemble the men with no sense of humour who insist on telling long funny stories in pubs. I talk about England v. Australia since 1876, until I fear that I am becoming a bore – except that nobody can really be boring about cricket.

My only practical cricketing distinction was playing in the city of Manaus, one thousand miles into the middle of the Brazilian Selvas. I had arrived there up the River Amazon, as doctor aboard a comfortable cargo-passenger ship from Liverpool. There is something reassuring, if ridiculous, about sitting down to your Sunday roast beef and Yorkshire amid Merseyside accents, at a temperature of 100 degrees Fahrenheit while floating at 20 mph though vivid, impassable, highly dangerous, bird-screeching jungle.

One of the junior engineers from Wallasey was even dottier about cricket than myself. He kept in his cabin pairs of sparkling, beautifully pressed flannels, lovingly whitened pads, bats oiled more conscientiously than the ship's machinery, gloves, stumps, bails, balls and an assortment of caps which would have shaken even a dandified Edwardian player. Each evening when he came off watch, the engineer would dress in full kit – pads and all, even a box – to practise shots before an invisible wicket against imaginary bowling on the poop. He made a diverting sight against the flaming tropical sunset. The captain wanted me to put him ashore into some Brazilian mental home, but I pointed out the inescapable oddness of sailors' hobbies. One of the mates was a keen gardener, his cabin was crammed with huge books on horticulture, but he had to grow all his highly bred roses, prize marrows and giant dahlias inside his own head.

Manaus gave a pleasant home-from-home feeling after Liverpool. It had an opera house and the same sort of trams. It was twice as hot and the air was full of large, noisy insects, each of which looked different and all of which bit. It held a sizable colony of cricket-mad Englishmen, who regarded our arrival as those at home welcomed the landing of the Australian tourists.

## Watching for Snakes

The cricket match against our ship's company was traditional. It was held on a field outside the city characterised by having no grass on it, and by the danger of chasing a ball over the boundary and being lost forever like Colonel Fawcett. The surface was cracked like a dropped eggshell, and fielders had to keep one eye on the ball and the other watching for snakes. We had to bring along the ship's carpenter with his tools to get the stumps in.

The engineer batted first, shining white like a bride and wearing a Harlequin cap. After studying his technique on the poop all across the Atlantic, I prepared for a display reaching towards Bradman or W.G. in his prime. The local bank manager opened with a slowish delivery very sportingly avoidingly a three-inch-wide fissure to the off. The batsman executed a delightful cover drive, but unfortunately after the ball had hit the wicket. Then it started to rain and as the locals agreed that it wouldn't stop at all for the next three months we decided to abandon the match as a draw.

That unhappy Harlequin-capped engineer was another purely theoretical cricketer. However humiliating on the field, at least it stimulates the imagination.

RICHARD GORDON, *Cricket '72*

To play at international level is the dream of all cricketers. Ian Ross achieved this aim; sadly his grandfather remained unimpressed.

# Called Up

As soon as I could walk my grandfather strapped me into a pair of oversized pads and began bowling gentle full-tosses and long-hops at me. His unspoken but obvious ambition was that his then one and only grandson would be the first member of the family to be capped for England, he having 'only' reached county standard.

There was no evidence of this particular strategy reaping any dividends as I struggled along in the 2nd XIs of school cricket, but I was able to cable him in October 1977 that finally his efforts had been vindicated and I had been selected for a national side. That he was not overly impressed by this achievement may have had something to do with the fact that the cable was sent from Nicaragua.

To get into the Nicaraguan cricket team was not difficult. There were only about fifteen people in the country who had ever held a cricket bat, and on one occasion a dog was included as number 11 in the misguided and desperate hope that it might prove its worth as an outfielder. With no domestic opposition we were forced to look to our neighbouring countries for a game. El Salvador and Costa Rica, being in a similar predicament, were delighted to oblige.

The pitches in Nicaragua and Costa Rica were in the grounds of British American Tobacco's local factories and reached a greenness unseen in the rest of Central America thanks to the use of tobacco dust as a fertiliser. Before each match a road mender would be 'encouraged' to divert his road roller over the pitch to generate sufficient bounce out of the normally soggy Bermudan grass.

But the pitch in the foothills outside San Salvador was the most picturesque. Purpose designed by the cricket-mad owner of a coffee *finca*, but built by labourers who had no idea what the game was about, it sloped sharply downhill across the pitch, giving a fine view of the hills across the valley. It was completely square so that a wicketkeeper standing back for a fast bowler was almost on the boundary rope. The highest score in any innings played there normally went to 'Extras'.

The standard of cricket played can best be described as erratic. Each country had its stalwarts; in Nicaragua a young Public Schools' XI fast bowler who was largely responsible for Costa Rica being 11 and 7 all out in consecutive matches; in Salvador an ex-county 2nd XI batsman who also took a number of wickets by virtue of bowling straight if slowly; in Costa Rica an ex-opening bat for Jamaica who admittedly by this time was in his seventies. There were also some useful club cricketers, but each country had a very long tail. The scorebooks of those matches record some very unorthodox performances.

The diligent reader will have noticed that this narrative is all in the past tense. The Civil War in Nicaragua and the political turmoil that followed in the region has led to the end of international cricket in that part of the world at least for the time being. The expatriates have left, as have some of the permanent residents with cricketing interests, the owner of the coffee *finca* died, and we never fostered any indigenous interest in the game. For those who stopped and stared we were no more than mad dogs and Englishmen out in the midday sun.

IAN ROSS, *Helsinki Cricketer*

An earlier report from Nicaragua seems
to bear out our previous correspondent.

# A Lazy Race

In that year (1886) a cricketer who had settled in Nicaragua
wrote: 'I have instituted your favourite old game, cricket, among the
natives, but they are such a lazy race that half an hour of it at a spin
completely does them up. I however wrote home to our directors and they
immediately kindly sent the officers out a complete outfit.

We call ourselves the Anglo–Nicaraguian team and I have no doubt you
would manage to put us all out in half an hour provided you escaped from
your innings alive, as the native bowling is very uncertain.'

*The Cricketer Annual, 1922–23*

Searching around for evidence of cricket
in British Honduras we came across this
delightful little piece concerning the hurricane that hit the colony in 1962.

# Hurricane Stopped Play

The recent disastrous hurricane which brought such de-
vastation and horror to the Crown Colony of British Honduras has
brought that small territory, whose coastline was discovered by Columbus
more than four and a half centuries ago, dramatically in front of the public
eye. It is not an inopportune moment, therefore, to glance at the cricketing
activities of the communities there, though it should be stated at once that
at no time has the cricket of British Honduras been of a standard to
effectively challenge the representative teams of other nations, even the
minor ones in the cricket brotherhood.

British Honduras is situated on the Caribbean Sea on the east coast of
Central America and is in extent about twice the size of Jamaica. So far as
opportunities for cricket are concerned, however, one must remember
that as much as ninety per cent of the land is covered with thick forests,
mountains or swampy soil and that, moreover, the population – which in
its entirety is only about one-third of that of Leicester – is a combination
descending from, inter alios, Negro slaves, native Indians and Spanish
buccaneers. In addition, its geographical position, described last year as

'one of the most remote and untravelled spots on the globe', has not contributed to the advancement of the colony's cricket.

## More than One Hundred Years

Cricket has never exactly flourished at any time in Central America, but compared with her neighbours Guatemala, Mexico, Honduras and Salvador, all with immensely larger populations, British Honduras can claim a veritable orgy of cricket activity stretching over a period of more than a hundred years. It was in the latter end of the eighteenth century that the country came under British control, and in the year 1862 – precisely a century ago – it was officially recognised as a colony associated with Jamaica. It will probably never be known for certain just how cricket was introduced into British Honduras, but when we recall that by the 1860s the game was already established (often for some years) in the Caribbean territories of Trinidad, Barbados, British Guiana and Jamaica, from which areas there was some measure of intercourse with British Honduras, it is clear that about this time too the game took hold there. The beginnings were certainly unorganised, as they were in many parts of the world, but from the names of the early pioneers we know that much of the credit for putting the game on its feet was due to the resident officials from Britain and the constabulary from Barbados, while of course ships from the Royal Navy, over a great many years, provided fresh, if not always substantial, opposition.

The first cricket club formed in British Honduras was called the Wanderers, and this still exists today in Belize. Until comparatively recent times the game was confined almost solely to the seaport capital Belize, a handsome city until so cruelly ravaged by nature in October. Belize, from all accounts, is no longer a city, and so violent and merciless was the force of the hurricane that struck it that very little escaped destruction. This must have a profound effect on the colony's cricket as well as on more basic issues, for virtually the greatest part of cricket interest manifested by British Hondurans came from Belize and Stann Creek, the second largest town, also hopelessly destroyed. The Belize Wanderers Cricket Club in 1888, when the annual subscription was the not inconsiderable sum of six dollars, had as many as forty-six playing members (as well as thirteen honorary ones) and was captained by an official, P. B. Wright (an Old Cheltonian); the team, then already some years old, always took the field in straw hats with a blue ribbon, on which was worked the monogram of the club. It was for the Wanderers that the highest individual score ever made in British Honduras was achieved – an innings of 105 by 'Sunt' Trumbach against their keenest rivals, the University. These two teams were for many years the two leading club sides in the country, and there used to be regularly played an annual fixture between them on 24 May (Empire Day) which was the outstanding sporting and social event of the year. The Wanderers, though the oldest club in the colony, and with an annually increasing membership, was not the only club in existence in the 1880s: there were at least six others, among them the University, Unity, Non Plus and Bon Accord. By 1890 there were about a dozen clubs.

It was not until the early years of the present century that the game blossomed out into an undeniable pastime in Belize. During the Governorship of Sir David Wilson (1897–1903) the happy idea of a Challenge Cup was introduced and proved extremely popular. Indeed, a feature of cricket in the colony since that time has been an annual competition for a cricket cup, usually named after a current Governor (e.g. Burdon's Cup, Kittermaster's Cup and Burns' Cup) which continued undiminished through both World Wars. In some years, more than one cup was competed for, and patrons of the game were not slow in showing their public-spiritedness.

The cricket ground at Newtown Barracks at Belize has always been the principal venue for cricket in British Honduras. There was a time, however, in 1903, when stringent regulations restricted the regular use of the ground with the result that cricketers were frustrated and a cloud grew over the game. This was soon happily removed by the action of the Governor, Sir Bickham Sweet-Escott, who, with Lady Sweet-Escott, gave their distinguished patronage to many cricket events in Edwardian days. His Excellency was a great lover of the game, and around this period many new clubs came into existence and matches were played between Officials and Unofficials and Single and Married Men. Army players, also, regularly held encounters.

## A Rare Pamphlet

Enthusiasm for cricket in British Honduras has not been so great in recent years as it was in the years between 1906 and 1931. A team from neighbouring Guatemala proposed making a visit to the colony in 1909, but the venture fell through. In the previous year there was issued in Belize a small pamphlet, now extremely scarce, entitled *A Concise Hint and Guide to Cricket*, by Isaiah Thomas, an amazing document couched in ridiculous bombast which, were it not for the general nature of the pamphlet, might make us seriously ponder on the following words: 'I cannot conceive how the majority of Cricketers nowadays are so much given to prejudice, and partiality, pretence and double-dealing, on the whole too susceptible to bribery, and flattery, self-conceit, ostentation, and folly.' At all events, progress continued to be made in the game and in 1914 there was established a Junior Cricket Competition, although standards remained somewhat low.

An event of some significance occurred in the middle of May 1928, when the first foreign team to visit British Honduras arrived at Belize. This was the Invincible Cricket Club from La Ceiba, an industrial city on the coast of the Republic of Honduras. The visitors played only one match, against the Cambridge Cricket Club of Belize, and the home side won. Interest in cricket in British Honduras was intense around this time, and the major stores of Belize often proclaimed in their windows the results of important local games within an hour or so of their ending. It was, therefore, all the more lamentable that cricket and so much else should have been disrupted by that earlier hurricane that struck Belize this century – in September 1931, causing so much death and havoc. The love of cricket prospered, however, so that exactly five years later the colony was able to entertain the Wembley Cricket Club from Jamaica, whose batsmen showed a style of cricket that taught the home players much. Of the three major games played against Belize, the Jamaicans won two and drew one, though there was high excitement when the visitors were put out in one of their innings for 37. The then Governor, Sir Alan Burns, always a keen supporter of cricket, presented the most successful Jamaican batsman, J. Marshalleck, with a beautiful figured mahogany bowl for his performances.

Another Jamaican team, led by Father Hugh B. Sherlock, then warden of Boys' Town, Kingston, visited British Honduras in December 1951, and proved far too strong for the local cricketers. The former interest in the game in the colony was not so much in evidence around this time, and during the 1950s constitutional and political issues assumed a greater prominence in the public mind. However, at the beginning of April 1960, for the first time in the history of the colony, an MCC side visited British Honduras for two one-day games of an exhibition nature at the end of the tour of West Indies. Fresh enthusiasm was aroused, and George Headley was called in from Jamaica to coach the British Hondurans in readiness for the visit. About four thousand people attended each of the two games at Newtown Barracks, MCC winning both very comfortably, even though they were without May, Cowdrey, Trueman and Statham. In the first match, against the Governor's XI, D. A. Allen scored 55 not out and Roy Swetman, in one of his rare turns with the ball, took three for 9. The MCC manager, Walter Robins, wearing a Free Foresters cap, captained MCC in the final game and opened the innings with Subba Row (58) against an All-Honduras XI (all local-born) captained by Telford Vernon, an all-rounder who played in England in 1954 for a Colonial Students' XI. The English left-hander, G. Pullar, batted right-handed, and MCC, in a light-hearted display, hit 227 before lunch and their final 277 in three hours.

MCC brought back with them a handsome plaque of the British Honduras coat of arms, presented by His Excellency the Governor, Sir Colin Thornley; and Subba Row brought back for himself a British Honduras five-cent piece, which he used when tossing as Northamptonshire's captain on his return. Walter Robins stated that he saw 'abundant talent' among the cricketers of British Honduras. It is to be hoped that that talent will not be stultified by the recent disaster there and that the colony, when it returns to normality, will continue to cherish those principles which have seen the game of cricket prosper for so many years.

IRVING ROSENWATER, *The Cricketer Spring Annual, 1962*

Our first report on the African continent
is of the local rules type. A very hungry
local rule.

# Mauled in the Deep

Frank Lane, noted writer on natural history, wrote of a
match at Nairobi in the days when the bush approached very near to the
town and a batsman drove a ball towards the boundary. As it was going
over the line a lion jumped out of the bush and began playing with the ball.
The fielders claimed 'lost ball', but the umpire insisted that, as the ball
could be seen, it wasn't lost. The batsmen crossed for an unrecorded
number of runs before enough men arrived to chase off the lion and
retrieve the somewhat chewed up ball.

GEORGE MELL, *This Curious Game of Cricket*

Next time the game of cricket you are
involved with is lost to rain, try this little
experiment. It seems to work very well.

# Kenyan Inferno

The first visit of the Kenya Kongonis to Tanga produced an
incident which is surely unique in the annals of cricket. The start of the
match was originally fixed for 9.30 a.m., but was delayed by heavy
overnight rain. It was anticipated that it would be possible to begin play at
10.30, but further rain made a start before luncheon seem out of the
question. It was then that one of the members of the Kongonis had an
inspiration, and on his suggestion twenty gallons of petrol were poured on
the wicket and set alight. There was a huge cloud of smoke and the pitch
resembled a scene from Dante's *Inferno*, or a smoke screen during a naval
battle – but the petrol did its work well and the intense heat dried the
wicket so effectively that it was possible to lay down the matting and begin
play before lunch. Perhaps it was not surprising that the wicket did a few
curious things.

*The Cricketer Annual, 1937–38*

Much of Africa has been starved of first-class competition. In this appeal from Kenya, reproduced from *The Cricketer Annual* of 1929–30, the lion rears its head again. This time to the good.

# Big Game Hunting

The MCC might seriously consider sending a side out here to play a few matches. No gate money could be taken, but a team of amateurs keen on big-game shooting might possibly be got together, and, in addition to cricket, get some of the finest shooting in the world, including lion, leopard, rhino, elephant, and buffalo, as well as most of the larger and smaller antelopes.

*The Cricketer Annual, 1929–30*

In some areas there seems to have been no problem over lions or wet wickets. Just shortages of manpower. But even this can be overcome.

# Ugandan Permutations

The Entebbe Sports Club foundation was formed by a handful of players hard put to reassert themselves so as to avoid the monotony of the XI playing the rest, their ingenuity achieved the permutations of Recent Arrivals v. Old Stagers, The World v. Old Indians, Anglo–Indians v. Anglo–Africans, the First Half of the Alphabet v. The Second Half. Two Africans, Long Boy and Short Boy, were allowed to go in at numbers 10 and 11. They never made more than one run between them.

E. W. SWANTON, *The World of Cricket*

You would think that when old national
enemies were forging a new life in another
continent they would forget old enmities.
If not in life, certainly on the cricket field.
These 'Nigerians', however, have not.

# Post-Umperial Problems

A city on the extreme northern border of Nigeria and an
ancient Sahara Desert trading town, Sokoto normally gets about fifteen
inches of rain a year, usually in the month of August. It has in the last
twenty years or so suffered from desert encroachment, and the pitch on
which I played for Kaduna State against Sokota State in 1979 effectively
showed the ravages of soil erosion. The wicket was a tarmac strip, the rest
of the field deep, very fine sand about five or six inches below the level of
the wicket. This made bowling a somewhat 'jumpy' event, and the sand
made batting difficult. The ball never ran more than six feet and the
fielders' main preoccupation was avoiding getting sand in their eyes. It
was a low-scoring game and, as I remember, Sokoto scored about eighty
all out in reply to Kaduna's ninety-two. However, the Sokoto coach was
an ex-Indian Test cricketer called Ghosh, who was known locally as
Harold for some completely unknown reason; there were also three other
Indians in the team and, importantly, an Indian umpire. Kaduna on the
other hand were captained by Mohammed Ilyas, a Pakistani, and there
were also two other Pakistanis and a Sri Lankan playing for Kaduna and,
not surprisingly, a Pakistani umpire. Kaduna batted first and I have never
played in a match where there were so many lbws, Ghosh got seven
wickets, six of which were lbw, and all at the Indian umpire's end. When
Sokoto batted, they quickly lost two wickets and Ghosh came in. He
quickly settled down and started to score. He must have got about thirty or
so when one of the Kaduna bowlers, Mehfooz, normally extremely
accurate, bowled an amazing over. Every ball was about a foot outside the
leg stump. Ghosh hit about three, but missed the fourth which hit him on
the pads. All the Pakistani players appealed 'rather loudly' but they
weren't quite as fast as the Pakistani umpire, whose finger was up – I'm
sure before they appealed. I was fielding in the covers, and Mohammed at
mid-off, as a 'somewhat disgruntled' Ghosh stalked off. When I voiced
my doubts about the decision to my captain, he smiled and said, 'Tony,
you must learn that any Pakistani umpire will give any Indian batsman out
before anybody appeals.'

TONY SHARP

Tom Lynn, newly arrived in Zaria, Nigeria, never pretended to be a fast-scoring,
let alone a whirlwind batsman; but
strange things can happen in far pavilions
of Africa.

# Whirlwind Innings

In Zaria, a town in northern Nigeria about 250 to 300 miles
south of the Sahara Desert, it does not rain very often. It generally, but not
always, rains once in May, quite regularly in June, July and August and
usually once in mid October. The cricket season runs from November to
April and in the fifteen years I have lived and played cricket in Zaria rain
has *never* stopped play except on one occasion. In 1975 Tom Lynn arrived
in Zaria. He was a moderate bowler but a good defensive bat. We were
short of an opening bat and Tom was pressed for service. On his own
admission he was not the most electric of openers, in fact in his entire
career he had never scored a fifty, until January 1977 when Zaria CC were
playing Ahmadu Bello University at Samaru (the University Campus).
The amazing happened, Tom prodded his way to a fifty. He had in fact got
52 and everyone cheered and the clapping was prolonged and enthusiastic. I am neither Christian nor Muslim, but somebody up there also gave a
cheer. A rather large whirlwind approached the ground, paper and
cardboard were whipped about twenty yards into the sky, it then rained,
very heavily as it does in the tropics, and as the wicket was a mat on top of
rolled mud, in about thirty seconds the mat was saturated and the ground
waterlogged. The game obviously had to be abandoned and we retired to
the bar. The amazing thing was that the rainstorm only covered an area
about a square mile. Tom Lynn, possibly fortunately, never scored
another fifty and is now, I understand, in Lesotho – hopefully fighting the
African drought in his own way.

TONY SHARP

The Horn of Africa would not be our ideal
concept of a cricketing-mad area.
Wrong again.
The Ethiopian Emperor Haile Selassie
commanded that the game be taught at all
secondary schools, and they even played a
game or two in British Somaliland. We
then take a big stride south to explore the
game in Madagascar, as it then was.

# War-time Cricket at Berbera

War-time cricket at Berbera, capital of what was then
British Somaliland, demanded extreme devotion and stamina. The British garrison (Army and RAF) appeared to number no more than a
hundred men – there must have been more, but my team never saw them.
Temperatures of about 120 degrees Fahrenheit in the shade, an asphalt
pitch positively bubbling in the heat and an outfield of very sharp gravel
substance – all tended to preserve the local team's unbroken record of
success against visiting sides. Not to mention the constant interruptions
for drinks – every thirty minutes, we quaffed beakers of cold but brackish
water (the beakers being enamel mugs or 'sawn-down' brown beer
bottles) drawn from a vast earthenware *chatti* carried on to the pitch by two
white-clad, smiling but breathless Somalis. We wrestled with other local
hazards – play with an ancient (dirty white) hockey ball, stumps of illegal
size and height, five tattered pads shared by both teams, and a series of
umpiring decisions geared in severity entirely to the military ranks and
popularity of the home side – Corporals and Privates could be given out
lbw or caught behind, but Majors and Captains never!

In a series of three exhausting matches starting at 9.30 a.m. (with a
break for tiffin and complete change of *dhobi* from 11.30 a.m. to 3.30
p.m.), we lost all of them comprehensively – the only bright spot being the
appearance of an immaculate officer of the Royal Engineers carrying
invitations for all to appear later for drinks and dinner. He turned out to be
Stanley Phebey, brother of Arthur Phebey of Kent, and no mean cricketer
himself – but he was content to entertain us in his rather spartan Mess and
not add to our failures in the field.

CHRISTOPHER BOX-GRAINGER, taken from *A Walk to the Wicket*

# Old Time Cricket in Madagascar

Many years ago, more than I care to remember, a Cricket Club was formed at Antananarivo, the capital of Madagascar, under the title of the 'Madagascar CC'.

I was on the way up country from Tamatave, the chief port – 220 miles in a Palanquin – at the time, but it was known at the capital that I was en route, and the promoters reckoned that, being an Englishman, I would be able to take a hand. I was selected to play in the first match, and when I at length arrived, sunburnt, flea- and mosquito-bitten, after a nine-day journey, was duly confirmed in my membership.

I found that two or three bats had been got over from Mauritius, and when it was known that I had got two cricket balls in my kit, the members were overjoyed, and set about having the other necessary tackle manufactured.

The wicketkeeping gloves were made out of two left-handed fencing gloves donated by the English Colonel in the native Army, and the pads were fashioned by the missionary ladies out of thin bamboo and Manchester calico.

The wicket stumps were built out of native spade handles, and the first match was played without bails.

I must say that we got more fun out of the game when we had to play with these improvised implements than we did later on when we received the correct outfit from Watson & Pilling.

The 'pitch' was situated on the Plain of Imahamasina, from which a steep hill arose, on the summit of which were placed picturesquely the Queen's Palace, the Prime Minister's Palace, and the Roman Catholic Cathedral.

The pitch was not *laid*. It consisted simply of a patch of plain earth, with here and there a tuft of grass, which the wily bowlers tried to use to advantage, sometimes with extraordinary results.

As there was no other cricket club within seven days' journey, teams, perforce, had to be chosen from the material at hand, and a very cosmopolitan lot they were, i.e. English, American, Creoles, Australians, South Africans, and Malagasy, comprising Merchants, Miners, Missionaries, Soldiers, Visitors and last, but not least, native boys.

The natives took to the game enthusiastically, and after a few team matches had been played, and a variation in the shape of a match East versus West Antananarivo (to vary the monotony of the ordinary 'Mr Thingummy's team v. Mr Whatshisname's'), a game was got up between the Club and 22 of the Malagasy, and right well did the boys play.

It was amusing to hear, and see, the native captain, Ralambo, set his field, interspersing his Malagasy directions with the English terms for the positions. A young fellow, wearing a straw top-hat, a long white calico shirt reaching his ankles, bare feet, and wrapped around with the inevitable *lamba* (a short toga), he would strike an attitude and shout, 'Hianao, Rafara, dia atao mid-on, ary hianao Ramanga atao short-slip hiany (i.e. You, Rafara, do mid-on and you, Ramanga, take short-slip).'

And so on until one very small urchin only was left, who came up anxiously, fearing to be overlooked in the distribution of the very large field. Ralambo regarded him sourly as being of little consequence, and dismissed him with a curt 'O ey, hianao atao back-stop!'

During our matches on Saturday afternoons we had big audiences of natives, who squatted on the ground, and seemed mightily interested in the game. They picked out any player who happened to have any peculiar characteristic, and roared with laughter at anything the least bit out of the normal, and at once 'christened' with deadly accuracy in their own language anyone indulging in any antic, studied or unconscious, the nick-name given being analogous with the action performed.

Sometimes a bullock of the humped and horned Zebu variety would gallop across the pitch, and scatter players and spectators alike. This episode never failed to raise a good deal of excitement, but what the native onlooker did not understand was why the Vazaha – the foreigner – did his own fielding, when he had a plethora of paid servants to do it for him.

On one occasion play was interrupted by an incident which became more or less an historical item. Doctor Rajaonah (son of the Governor of Tamatave, whom in later years I had the sorrow to see executed for high treason), who had taken his medical degree at Edinburgh, and was forced to return and marry the PM's daughter, had been arrested on some trumped-up political charge, and was brought right across our pitch by palanquin bearers, as he was being taken into durance vile down South.

The French war of conquest broke up the Club, and the members returned to their old love, hard-court tennis, but nevertheless, whilst it lasted the cricket was thoroughly enjoyed by all kinds and conditions of members, notwithstanding the disadvantages of crude tackle and primitive pitch.

After the French occupation, the military authorities formed a sports club, and built a Velodrome, and the Commander in Chief asked the writer to try to get his officers interested in the game, with a view to attaching it to the new club, Le Sport Club de Tananarive, but as the aides-de-camp who were told off to take lessons did not trouble to dismount from their horses, it was not found possible to start Criquette-à-Cheval and the project fell through.

WILLOUGHBY TURNER, *The Cricketer Spring Annual 1933*

Could stout Cortez, staring on the Pacific
with his eagle eye, have even wildly sur-
mised the wealth of endearing cricket
anecdotage and lore the Ocean would
contribute to the literature of the game?
Rowland Bowen, writing in the 1940s,
begins our survey.

# Pacific Round-up

The Navy has been responsible as much as, if not more than,
anyone else for propagating the game among the Pacific Islands, and it
was in this period that cricket in Fiji, and Samoa and Tonga, and in other
islands first began to come to notice. Even before the cession of the Fiji
islands to Britain, a club had been formed in Levuka, and within a few
years Fijians themselves were playing the game. It made great progress
towards the end of the period, largely owing to the enthusiasm of J. S.
Udal, a colonial judge and a well-known cricketer in England before his
appointment, and it was just after the period ended that Fiji went on its
first overseas tour, to New Zealand. P. A. Snow has written a fascinating
account[1] of the game in those islands, and for any lover of the game, or the
Pacific, his details are extremely rewarding.

Not so far away as distances are measured in the Pacific, there lie the
Samoan Islands, at this time and almost to the end of the period, another
independent kingdom. Here too the game caught on amongst the native
inhabitants, and became a fever, of such danger to the country's economy
that it had to be prohibited by law. This prohibition has been reimposed at
later times in the history of the islands, when economic circumstances, or
the results of a hurricane have compelled it. The reason is simple: the
Samoan version of cricket provided for an entire village playing another
village, all of them fielding. Batsmen queued up to go in, the head of the
queue a pace or two from the batsman still in, waiting to rush to the wicket
when he should be out – for, if he did not get there in time, he might be
bowled by the opposing bowler before he had time to take his stance! An
entirely delightful version of the game, and an excellent substitute for war!

There is a lot of cricket played elsewhere in the Pacific: local varieties
such as that played in New Caledonia, or that played more widely in
Samoa and other islands, as well as the accepted version. Samoan cricket
can still take up the time and manpower of whole villages, and can still, as
over seventy years ago, require the authorities to ban it to get any work
done. The normal version is played there too, and is of a reasonable

---

[1] *Cricket in the Fiji Islands* (New Zealand, Whitcombe & Tombs Ltd, 1949)

standard in terms of club cricket. But the cricketing power in the Pacific is Fiji, which has sent several teams on tour to New Zealand since the last war, resuming a pre-1914 precedent, and which have attained a high standard, and not only that, an approach to the game which in itself was always enough to draw expectant, and duly satisfied crowds. One team has been to Australia since before the first war, and beat a strong New South Wales team in a one-day match.

ROWLAND BOWEN, *Cricket: a History of its*
*Growth and Development throughout the World*

**Cricket on Fiji is far from being a novelty. We learn from Bill Frindall's piece below that it dates back to 1881, when W.G. was still in his early thirties. Certainly the island has had time to accumulate some staggering records, as the master statistician recounts. Consider the incredible over delivered by Saisasi Vunisakiki one warm Pacific day in 1940!**

## Frindall on Fiji

In the South Sea archipelago of Fiji, cricket is still a very powerful force. Formerly the inhabitants had the attributes that make a good fast bowler: they were hostile and had strong cannibalistic tendencies. Cricket is thought to have been introduced to these two hundred and fifty scattered islands in January 1874, when immigrant enthusiasts formed a club at Levuka, then the capital. Having superb natural agility and brilliantly fast reflexes, the Fijians quickly took to the game with a fierce and simple relish; their creed was that it was a game only for the hardest hitters and fastest bowlers; there have been few Fijian spinners. Before the locals were widely absorbed into the game, European settlers played the earliest matches against passengers of visiting ships on the Sydney to San Francisco run. In 1881 they played a team from HMS *Bacchante* that contained a young midshipman – Prince George, who later became King George V.

In 1895, Attorney-General J. S. Udal, a former Somerset player, led the first Fijian tour to New Zealand. His side, which included six Fijian chiefs, won four of its eight matches. However, such tours were rare. Playing standards failed to improve until 1946, when the Fijian Cricket Association was formed and promoted the game on an interracial basis; previously, European teams had been segregated from those containing

Fijians and Indians. In 1948, Philip Snow, a colonial service administrative officer, led a fully representative team to New Zealand.

The Fijian members of Snow's party were marvellous crowd pullers. They looked sensational on the field with their bare feet, bushy haloes of hair and wearing sulus, the traditional calf-length skirts, split up one side to the waist.

One of the most appealing players was an outstanding batsman who mercifully appeared in the scorebook merely as 'I. L. Bula'. His real name, and there are several versions of it, is a cricket record in itself: Ilikena Lasarusa Bulamainavaleniveivakabulaimainavavaoalakebalau, which makes the name of India's fine spinner S. Venkataraghavan (a meticulous commentator's nightmare) seem almost abrupt. Bula's resounding strokeplay and nimble footwork brought him 1,011 runs in 29 innings on the tour; his 246 is also the highest score in Fijian cricket. Good as it is, this record looks mundane beside that of the finest bowling feat there. In 1940, Saisasi Vunisakiki took a wicket with every delivery in an eight-ball over – an achievement that should stay in the record books forever. Fijian grounds are charming but poorly appointed, apart from Albert Park, Suva and Nasau Park, Levuka. Albert Park has a pleasingly diversified setting; it is surrounded by the Grand Pacific Hotel, a line of imposing Government buildings, botanical gardens and a palm-hung soapstone cliff.

BILL FRINDALL, *The Cricketing Nations*

**We have already failed to wrap our tongues around the full name of Fiji's most outstanding batsman. Here he comes again at roughly the same length but with a slightly different spelling supplied by *The Cricketer*. We have no intention of umpiring in such discrepancies. The simple fact is that Fiji holds the record for cricketers' names.**

# Stumped for Length

### The Longest Name in Cricket

The outstanding cricket personality in Fiji is a big Fijian who boasts the name of Ilikena Lasarusa Bulamaineiilikenamainavaleniveivakabulaimainakulalakebalau. It roughly means 'Returned alive from Nakula Hospital at Lakemba Island in the Lau group'. Lau is a group of islands within the Colony of Fiji and almost half-way to the Kingdom of Tonga. The story goes that Bula. . .'s grandfather was seriously ill at the same hospital when the infant Ilikena was born. The news of his birth delighted the old gentleman so much that he made a quick recovery and was soon able to go home to admire and christen his grandchild, and future big hitter.

**Bula's Twenty-two Sixes**
On 17 January last year Bula hit up the record Fiji individual score of 246 in 173 minutes out of a total of 435. During this hurricane innings he hit twenty-two sixes and ten fours. Bula set up his record in a Suva 'A' grade match for his club, Queen Victoria School Old Boys, against Samabula. One of the unlucky bowlers was the leading fast bowler of the 1948 touring side, Isoa Logavatu.

**A Hit from Saturday into Sunday**
In a country renowned for its big hitters, it is perhaps appropriate that it was once possible in Fiji to hit a ball from Saturday into Sunday and for the fielder to return the ball from the boundary (on Sunday) to the wicketkeeper, who received the ball from a smart throw-in on the same Saturday as he saw the big hit. At a place called Waiyevo on the island of Taveuni passes the 180° Meridian (International Date Line), but the Date Line was, by International agreement, officially bent out to sea, presumably to avoid such complications.

*The Cricketer Spring Annual, 1960*

Religion, alcohol and Fijian cricket.

# Confessions of a Tenderfoot

A large temple, built on a mound of coral rock and sand-stone, and the home of the old-time human sacrifice, has been converted into a pavilion, and a pitch, clipped and rolled by the natives with all the care of a Lord's groundsman, has been railed off in the centre of the town enclosure. Here, almost every day, Ratu Kadavu coaches members of his team at the nets or tries them out in a practice game, the ground being meanwhile surrounded by an enthusiastic throng of spectators. The team's fielding is wonderfully quick and clean; in the long field especially, their swiftness in saving boundaries and reaching apparently impossible catches is very marked. Their bowling, too, is dangerously true. One member of the team, a wiry giant of six feet two, can take the ball and bowl down any stump that is indicated.

When the players get thirsty, one of their number climbs a coconut palm and throws down some green nuts, their milk and half-formed kernels being extremely refreshing.

*Kava*, however, is the universal drink of Fiji, and as such is never prepared without fitting ceremony. When, after an hour's hard work at the nets, Ratu Kadavu suggested a refresher of Fiji grog, as he irreverently terms his national beverage, all the ancient rites associated with its brewing were bound to be observed; and it is by these little ceremonies, these returns to the ways of their fathers, that one may catch glimpses of the real life of the Fijian people, lying hidden, but not dead, beneath the as yet thin veneer of civilisation that is spreading over their land.

Leaving the present-day balls and bats, stumps and pads, we entered Ratu Kadavu's native house by a door four feet high, and plunged into the past. The walls of this dark, lofty room were hung with *tapa* (the bark of a native tree beaten to the thinness of paper), traced with weird patterns in vegetable dyes. The floor was covered three or four deep with mats, some of which were as finely woven as a panama hat, and on these the natives sat in semicircles, the women well in the background, while I, as the guest of honour, was assigned a seat on a raised dais at the end of the room, and did my best to look worthy of the position.

The *Yangona*, a nubbly root from which the *kava* is made, was then brought in, cut into fair-sized pieces, and given to three or four of the prettiest girls in the town, who, after washing out their mouths, sat in a circle about the *kava* bowl and solemnly chewed the root into a conglomerate and juicy mass, their slow and laboured mastication, accompanied with bulging cheeks and expressionless faces, exactly resembling the cud-chewing of a contented cow. When sufficient root had been chewed, it was placed in a *kava* bowl, and a coconut shell or two of water poured over it and squeezed thoroughly with the hands until every drop of juice was extracted and mixed with the water. By this time the beverage looked like dirty dish-water, and when white rags were drawn through it by way of straining, one could hardly help speculating on the chances of a stray spoon or fork coming to light at any moment. A brimming coconut shell was then poured out and brought to me by a very old man, whose skin was withered and scaly like a snake's.

My name was then announced, and to the accompaniment of clapping hands and guttural grunts – knowing that to pause in the middle of drinking is considered an act of grave discourtesy to the host – I managed to drain the shell at a draught, to the huge delight of everyone present.

I had heard a great deal about the effects of *kava* on those unaccustomed to it, and half an hour after that ceremony I began to experience them for myself.

At first I fancied I was suffering from a bilious attack. A heaviness seemed to have descended upon me and bright pin-pricks of light flashed up before my eyes. Then, quite suddenly, my knees commenced to tremble and bend unexpectedly at crucial moments. We were again at the nets, and I was forced to go and sit under a tree to recover.

Ratu Kadavu was batting, and every now and then looked in my direction, smiling broadly. This struck me as rather unsympathetic, and, as my head was perfectly clear, I struggled to my feet and stumbled towards the bowling crease. Ratu Kadavu laughed, and with that laugh came to me a full realisation of what was amiss. It annoyed me; surely I could stand as much of that dish-water as the next man, I thought. At any rate, I would be avenged! I seized a ball, set my teeth, and prepared to put on plenty of pace. The pace was there, but the ball went outside the net! Also, my knees collapsed completely, and when I looked up from the grass it was to see, through a perfect constellation of shooting lights, Ratu Kadavu seated in an undignified attitude before the wickets convulsed with uncontrollable laughter.

An hour later I had quite recovered and was waving farewell from the stern of the launch to Ratu Kadavu Levu, Prince of Fiji, and best of sportsmen and good fellows.

RALPH STOCK, *Confessions of a Tenderfoot*

Cricket is heartily embraced by both sexes on the picturesque Tuvaluan island of Funafuti. Here, according to E. K. Brown, the Hambledon bat is still in fashion. Let us hope that Civilisation's access continues to be restricted to one flight a week and the 'sporadic journeyings' of the cargo ship *Nivanga*.

# Funafuti Goings-on

With only one flight a week in and out of Funafuti, the airstrip is used more as a focal point for the island's leisure activities than as a runway. It is about 250 yards wide and fringed picturesquely with coconut palms and banana and breadfruit trees. The grass is long and wiry and the ground hard and bumpy, with odd concrete patches still remaining. Inter-island games are not possible as there is no means of communication except by the sporadic journeyings of the *Nivanga*, a small cargo ship from Suva.

Before Independence, Vaitupu was the capital, and there was once a good cricket ground there, made under the direction of a cricketing headmaster of the secondary school. This ground has now fallen into decay.

My early enquiries about cricket on the airstrip elicited the information that the ladies were as enthusiastic as the men, if not more so. Play starts about seven in the morning, for by midday it is extremely hot, and darkness falls as early as 6.30. The climate varies little throughout the year; rain can stop play and there is no difference of temperature between the cricket and football seasons.

Football is played in a league with teams of such fascinating names as

Combined Devils, Smokie, Jungle Boys and Dumbling. Portable goal-posts are carried out. When football palls there is a close season of several months, but when I was there in March, cricket and football were both being played.

On the first Saturday morning I made my way to the air-strip at seven to find that two ladies' games were in progress, plus a men's game and two football matches. It was an astonishing sight, like a scene from a London park transferred to a coral atoll of only just over two square kilometres. The two women's sides, Senala and Alapi, were just beginning separate local practices. I was advised to seek out Apikaila Papapamau of the Philatelic Bureau, the leading enthusiast and organiser, for further information.

The game played by the ladies originated in Samoa and there are many variations on the orthodox game played by the men. The wicket is a single stump and the bat is shaped like that used by the Hambledon Men. The ball, the size of a golf ball, is skilfully made with a round pebble as core, wrapped round with layers of pandanus leaves. There can be up to three or four runners who have long rods like fishing poles; the batswoman does not run. The young and the not-so-young, dressed in bright colours, with T-shirts, trousers or skirts, all took part, and the fielders, about two dozen of them, positioned themselves apparently according to their own incli-nation. There was a scorer with a notebook and pencil, but what she recorded I could not fathom.

There was utter confusion at times, with arguments and stand-up or sit-down strikes; whenever a wicket fell there was a jubilant song and dance. There was much good-humoured barracking and everyone was enjoying it all immensely. I was the only man watching and the ladies were surprised at my interest. They probably put it down to the oddity of a *palangi* – a foreigner.

E. K. BROWN, *Wisden Cricket Monthly*, February 1981

'Cricket legitimises the demarcation by men of yet another time and space where they can be free of women and united with other men,' wrote Joan Smith in the *New Statesman* recently, thus securing herself a niche in *Private Eye*'s W.I.M.M.I.N. fea-tures. Heaven knows what she would make of the following true story!

## Sex Warfare in the Solomon Islands

We were not so lucky on Trobriands Islands in the Solomon group. Time is not a vital factor in the Solomons, and matches tend to drift on for two or three days until they are finished. I had managed to become involved in a game with some of the men from the island which was sauntering along gently until it was brought to an abrupt halt by some angry women. About forty of them invaded the pitch brandishing clubs and other weapons. The men surrendered at once and the women then proceeded to play a match between themselves. It transpired that the society of the island was matriarchal; the women ran the villages and the men worked in the forest and fields. The women ruled and therefore their games took precedence over the men's. They wanted to play, and the presence of white fellows from England made no difference to the fact that in the natural order of things their game was the more important. Their one concession to the occasion was to entertain us later to a magnificent feast, resplendent with suckling pigs, plantains and all else.

CHRISTOPHER BOX- GRAINGER, taken from *A Walk to the Wicket*

In one of the first of Britain's post-war economic crises, weekday football was banned to encourage factory attendance, but cricket was exempted, possibly because Prime Minister Clement Attlee had a soft spot for the game. According to the celebrated cricket historian, F. S. Ashley-Cooper, Samoa was once faced with a similar problem. Only here there could be no doubt as to which game was plunging the island into economic peril.

## Cricket Outlawed!

The game seems to have been introduced here [in Samoa] by HMS *Diamond* about the year 1884, and the natives, who took to it readily, at once saw there was much room for improvement. Matches of two hundred aside took place, with four or five umpires and three batsmen at each end, the contests lasting for weeks. Work was neglected, and steps had to be taken to compel the natives to return to reason. Men who played were expelled from Church, and the King had to issue a special decree. As the latter fact has been doubted, it may be well to reproduce the actual Proclamation:

## THE LAW REGARDING CRICKET
### To all the Districts of Samoa, Notice

1. It is strictly prohibited for a village to travel and play cricket with another village.
2. It is strictly prohibited for two villages to play cricket together.
3. It is also prohibited for a village to play cricket among themselves.
4. Should any village or district fail to keep this law in any respect, they will be fined a sum not exceeding forty-five dollars, or in default be sent to jail for three months with hard labour.

Residence of the King, Apia,      Malietoa, The King of Samoa.
    June 20, 1890

F. S. ASHLEY-COOPER, *Cricket Highways and Byways*

**Thankfully the game is no longer banned, and the Samoans are free to play their hearts out. Indeed there is even a suggestion that cricket could be part of a larger mating game.**

# Samoan Rituals

Samoan cricket has to be seen to be believed. It is rich in laughter, has elements of farce, echoes of tribal warfare, a touch of the Glee Club, gives a nod or two in the direction of MCC laws and is played in noisy enthusiasm against exotic backgrounds of blue lagoons, waving palms, rubber trees and the beautiful feathery *tamalingi* with its red flowers.

It is a game that is played with pleasure by men and women equally. In Apia, the capital of Western Samoa, it is played on an area of land recovered from the sea called the Eleelefou. The concrete wicket is slightly longer than ours, and four feet wide. It is raised about three inches off the ground, which makes no-balling virtually impossible. The bats are three-sided and forty-four inches long, tapering to a rounded handle bound in coconut cord. Individual marks in bright colours are painted on the base part.

Some people are reminded of baseball when they first see the bats, but I see them as tribal clubs, smashing the hard rubber ball which the players make themselves from strips of raw rubber off the trees, as they used to crack the skulls of their Tongan or Fijian enemies. There are no bails as the strong sea breezes would keep shipping them off.

The teams are twenty-a-side and it is a picturesque sight when they take the field in their colourful *lavalavas* (cotton wrap-around skirts worn by both sexes), wearing T-shirts and bare-footed. Each side brings its own umpire. In the harbour tall-masted yachts gently sway at anchor, and overlooking the town and the pitch is the thickly wooded Mount Vaea where Robert Louis Stevenson lies in his simple tomb on the summit in the paradise he made his own.

The batting side does not repair to the pavilion when the game begins, as there is no such place. Instead the other eighteen players sit in a semicircle in the position of the slips. Most of the fielders being on the leg-side as the game proceeds – runs are called points – the seated batting side will break into song; sad traditional melodies or war chants accompanied by handclapping. Leading the musical entertainment is 'the teacher', a chorus master-cum-cheerleader of charisma, and whatever he does the rest of the team dutifully follows. He also has a whistle which he blows from time to time and he will go into rhythmical gyrations as if on a dance floor, followed by his team.

Now it might be thought that this was done to encourage the batsmen at the wicket or to put the bowlers out of their stride. Not a bit. It was just done out of Polynesian joie de vivre. But the fielding side had their weapon also.

The 'teacher' would blow his whistle, leap in the air with whoops, twisting and turning in impromptu dance and grimacing like a gargoyle. He would end by jumping up and clapping his hands above his head with his team emulating him. This, too, was an expression of uninhibited joy and had nothing to do with intimidation.

When a wicket fell, however, the performance was intensified with leaping and shouting and laughter and with the more athletic doing cartwheels and somersaults. It made me think that Derek Randall might have visited this pearl of the Pacific; he would be in his element in this game.

The batsmen have two stances. Some will rest the bat over their shoulders as if waiting to brain some creatures emerging from the swamps, while others point it to the ground like a golfer lining up for a prodigious drive; and both men and women, perhaps a little inelegantly, thrust the folds of their *lavalavas* between their muscular thighs before taking guard.

All the bowlers are fast and they only take three or four paces before hurling the ball down. Women bowl underarm. The ball is always well pitched up, usually middle and leg, and rises sharply. Sometimes the batsmen were hit in the tenderest of places. As they scorn such aids as helmets, boxes, gloves and pads, I winced for them. But they seemed unaffected and just laughed when they were hit.

In fact, whatever the players did they laughed in doing it; dropping a catch, being out first ball, missing a run-out or whatever were causes for loud laughter, and they laughed just as loudly when making a mighty hit into the sun or into the long grass in the outfield where fielders were up to their waist in couch grass.

The ball is bowled from whichever end it lands – there are no overs –

and the bowlers are also the wicketkeepers. Although most of the batting reminded me of the village blacksmith having a bash after a skinful of scrumpy, the other aspects of the game were more skilful. Men and women throw straight and hard – learned from their childhood when they threw stones at tins and other objects – and they all seem to have a flair for wicketkeeping, going through the motions of whipping off imaginary bails like a Rodney Marsh.

Batsmen always go for the big hit as it is too tiring to run for singles in the heat. When it was time for a break – the lunch or tea interval – both teams sat on the grass drinking soft drinks and eating biscuits and chatting.

One of the happy sights in Apia between 4 p.m. and 6.15 p.m. is to see a few hundred women of all ages and shapes and in a variety of costumes playing cricket on the Eleelefou. The scene is a happy blend of colour, noise and enthusiasm, and when it comes to the histrionics of the game the men pale beside the women.

The woman 'teacher' will grimace grotesquely, thrusting her arms to her side and waggling her fingers. Then she will bend her knees, roll her buttocks, kick out in puppet-like movements, straighten up and jump up and down as if demented, all the time blowing her whistle. Then she will kick her left leg as if getting rid of a persistent admirer and leap into the air with both arms extended; she was followed in all her actions by the rest of the team.

On occasions the performance would end with the women facing the men and lifting up their *lavalavas* for what could have been a full frontal if they had not been wearing a kind of cut-down cotton long johns. It must have frightened the living daylights out of their enemies in the old days.

The men's cricket season has now ended and I saw the last game between the town area and the village of Ifilele Aasa. The town team had fifteen Mormon bishops playing for it and one of the umpires was Bishop Afamasaga Laulu, who is also the tribal chief of Fasitootai. He was a splendidly dignified figure in his creamy jacket, ecclesiastical purple *lavalava* and his clipboard.

As each side had won a game they played a decider – but only fifteen players each this time to shorten the proceedings – and the game was won by the visitors.

Last Saturday saw the start of the women's cricket season with a game between Vineula ladies, of Apia, and Miliemo. The home team scored 60 points, the visitors 24. So it was a comfortable win of 36 points for the locals, ranging from slim-legged, doe-eyed schoolgirls to muscular, big-busted and broad-beamed ladies.

Although Samoan cricket is fun from beginning to end, it once had a tragic sequel. In a match not far from Apia a visiting batsman was given out when the ball was caught by a young spectator. The batsman protested, but the home umpire, proud of his young brother who had made the catch, stuck to his decision. The batsman killed him with one savage swipe of his bat.

But things like that do not happen today. Samoan cricket seems to make many of its rules as it goes along. But who cares? It has a logic of its own, and so long as it is an occasion for so much laughter and pleasure long may these Polynesian 'flannelled fools' in their cotton *lavalavas* make a spectacle of themselves and make an entertainment for us.

CHRISTOPHER BOX-GRAINGER, taken from *A Walk to the Wicket*

**We have been accused of giving credence to one or two fishy cricketing yarns, and this is certainly the fishiest of them all. Yet it carries the authority of the 'Thunderer' itself.**

# 'Caught Fish'

Sir, Mr Thornton Berry's anecdote (of a half-pound grayling killed by a six-hit) reminds me of a strange incident in far Sohar, where we were wont to peg down a mat on the seashore and play cricket as an antidote for nostalgia.

The last-wicket stand on a memorable afternoon was troublesome indeed, for the temperature was 110 degrees, maybe more; and umpiring I found less pleasant than sitting near a well under some palms.

At last a ball was hit for six into the sea; but it fell not into the sea, for it was swallowed by a shark.

I thought of the blessed shade under the palms, and gave the man 'out'. 'c. Fish b. Birkat Ullah' was duly entered in the score book by a soldier clerk.

I am, Sir, your obedient servant,
R. Townshend Stephens

R. TOWNSHEND STEPHENS, letter to *The Times*, 12 July 1934

**Two stories about Papua, New Guinea. Is this still quite cricket?**

# Bending the Rules in Papua

Native cricket in the Tropics differs considerably from the game as played in accordance with MCC rules and under Western conditions. For the players wear little more than is demanded by the laws of decency, the torrid climate making clothes superfluous, while the pitch is framed in palm-trees, green parakeets shrieking in the foliage, and monkeys jumping from one trunk to another, chattering and gibbering as they leap. Insects, far larger than the European variety, noisily chirp and buzz in the long, coarse grass, and, when the short twilight sets in, fire-flies are on the wing. All, in fact, is animation.

Nor is the game confined to the chosen teams. At first, eleven natives take the field, it being their commendable intention to play in accordance with the instructions furnished by the good missionaries, who, years ago, introduced cricket to innumerable converts – and heathens. . . . But, wearying of fielding, point, cover-point, long-stop and others betake themselves to cool groves, there to pluck the scarlet hibiscus, twining it about woolly heads and bronze necks and arms. Or, overcome by hunger and thirst, since fielding under a blazing sun causes the mind to wander in a more interesting direction, the original eleven dwindles considerably, the adjacent coconut trees having the fielders' attention. A small boy, naked save for a diminutive waist-cloth, swarms up a tree and shakes down the nuts. The milk is greedily swallowed; the 'meat' is devoured, unless golden-yellow bananas are preferred. Sometimes, indigestion setting in, the *gourmands* are handed over to the coloured doctor, a practitioner whose methods are strange. A hot brick, for example, is applied to the stomach.

The depleted team is quickly reinforced, every absentee being replaced by several volunteers. Indeed, there may be as many as twenty natives fielding, such is the enthusiasm for the Papuan game; even the spectators, old and young, chase after the ball. The onlookers also relieve the bowler, the last-named cheerfully retiring when politely requested to do so. Very obliging.

Men, women, boys and girls form the respective elevens. The players' bodies are lavishly smeared with coconut oil, flowers are stuck in the hair, the young girls (some of whom are well favoured) sport tinkling shell earrings, necklaces and bangles. All laugh at hits and misses, for in merry Papua everything is a jest. Consequently, the hero who carries his bat for a century and the batsman who is bowled first ball are greeted with laughter. A joyous crew are the Papuans.

Conversation is part and parcel of the game. The bowler, with arm uplifted, pauses to discuss local politics with the batsman, the fielders joining in the discussion. The spectators, anxious to display their powers of oratory, and quitting the shade for the sunlight, take part in the debate. After half an hour's chatter and jabber, the captain, remembering that cricket is the business of the moment, claps his hands, berates the players, and orders the intruders off the field. Laughter follows, with a few remonstrations thrown in, the orators hating to be deprived of life's greatest pleasure. Eventually the spectators withdraw.

Occasionally a greybeard, tired of looking on, expresses a wish to play. Age being honoured in the Tropics, the venerable man is handed a bat, the batsman whom he ousts willingly running for him each time the ball is hit, since the patriarch usually is somewhat unsteady on his pins. The bowler must bowl slowly and wide of the wicket – etiquette demands the amiable sacrifice.

Scoring is a strange affair, the losing side increasing its score by adding sufficient runs to the scoring book to render defeat honourable. Nor does the winning eleven raise any objection; provided the addition is discreet the winners are thoroughly satisfied. The oddly-formed ball is of wood, and fielders, not caring to risk a hard knock, make no attempt to stop the dangerous missile; they much prefer to let the ball speed its course – a compromise which sends up the score amazingly. The bats, which are not unlike small paddles, vary in size, players consulting their own taste. The stumps, of which there are six, even seven, also touch each other, while bails never have been, and probably never will be, used. When the missionaries first introduced the game, nicely-turned bails were procured from England, to immediately disappear. Years afterwards they decorated the hut of a chief, who, declining to forsake the creed of his ancestors, worshipped them. Upon the devout Papuan lately succumbing to the well-meant attentions of a native 'medicine-man', the bails were buried with him. Such was his last dying wish.

Every now and then one village challenges another. The day is arranged to suit the convenience of the visitors, who, arriving early in the morning, are regaled with coconut milk, garlanded with hibiscus, and begged to make themselves at home. They do so by falling asleep, the walk in the sun having proved fatiguing. Eventually the captain awakes and, collecting his scattered faculties, remembers the business that has brought him so far from home. Arousing the slumbering team, he and the rest of the male eleven seek the pitch, patiently to await the arrival of the home team. Finally, their opponents, who have also been wrapt in slumber, turn up, and play begins.

The inter-village match is governed by odd rules. Should the captain fancy a player on the opposite side, offering in exchange one of his own men, no objection is raised. If a batsman prefers to finish the innings at leisure, he temporarily favours the 'shade of sheltering palm', returning to the wicket later on in the day. Should the hard, wooden ball catch a visiting player on the shin or funny-bone the spectators must not laugh, it being considered rude to indulge in hilarity at the expense of a guest. Only when a mishap befalls an onlooker may unlimited mirth prevail.

Play having come to an end, the winners and losers are feasted. A pig is killed by a tremendous blow on the head, roasted whole over a wood fire, strewn with flowers, and quickly devoured. The Papuans being hearty feeders, the 'medicine-man' often is called in during the night. The hot brick cure does the trick.

GEORGE CECIL, *Cricketer Spring Annual, 1928*

**The mating urge raises its head again in this further report on the game in Papua. A sociologist may be able to see a connection here with our own Eton v. Harrow match in the period when it attracted the flower of the débutantes. All the same it's obviously a far cry from St John's Wood!**

# Matchmaking Fixtures

The turn-of-the-century missionary who introduced cricket to the Trobriand Islands, off the south-east coast of Papua New Guinea, scored a resounding duck. It was intended to steer the natives' celebrated sexual energies into channels more acceptable to the Church, but he did not reckon on his flock's sporting instincts.

When the menfolk want to bowl a maiden over, they play cricket. Happily, the season coincides with the July yam harvest, a prolonged fertility festival.

It is a sight to stir the stumps of MCC members in the Long Room at Lord's. Trobriand cricketers dress as they would for war – painted faces, feathers, bodies glistening with coconut oil to ensure courage, and ankle-bands to promote speed of reaction. Little else is worn except for a jockstrap made from the skin of a betelnut tree. One fashion-conscious Trobriand wears a codpiece made from a mackerel-tin wrapper.

Before the game, bats are painted with war colours of black and white and, by magic, endowed with potent hitting powers. Once the game is under way, spells are used by bowlers to swerve and swing the ball and mystify the batsmen. In retaliation, the batting side's magicians make the bowler's arm go limp and protect the wicket with an invisible shield.

When a batsman is bowled, the game is interrupted as the fielders – often sixty a side – celebrate with dancing and chants of 'Stupidity! Stupidity!' If a batsman is caught, they chant 'My hands are PK' – PK being the islands' favourite brand of chewing gum, sticky like the hands of the fielders. Scoring is done by plucking the leaves from a coconut frond. It hardly matters, because etiquette demands that the home team win, but only by a narrow margin.

Like ritual warfare, cricket gives the men the chance to flaunt their masculinity before an audience of admiring girls who favour a fetching outfit rather like a diminutive skirt with no knickers. After the game, spectators and sportsmen often pair off and vanish into the bush for a post-match discussion.

Not quite cricket, but a few Trobriand adaptations could do a lot to improve falling attendances over here.

MICHAEL MACKINTYRE, *The New Pacific*
(Brought to our attention by Richard Edwards)

For sheer enthusiasm you can't beat the
Melanesians. Have you ever fielded in a
heavy surf?

# Leg Breakers in Melanesia

The boys are immensely keen on house matches (five
houses in the school). They are limited to two and a half hours, into which
we have to get two innings aside. We just do it, making 250 to 300 runs
in the time. This is because all Melanesians think every ball should be hit
for six, and if they can't do it, they try to. (I am myself a miserable
stone-waller, an object of universal detestation, but what wouldn't I give
to hit sixes!) We have the most glorious finishes, closing with the utmost
daring to get a win, and abhorring draws. In the final last year the Gave
(Crab) house had to get 108 in twenty-one minutes. They just did it! They
all take guard most carefully, but purely as ritual; they then stand a bit to
leg and prepare to hit. If anyone gets a nasty knock from a hard hit, the ball
is brought and rubbed on the sore spot, and all is well. They are good
bowlers, and grand fieldsmen; a possible catch is hardly ever missed, close
in, or a high one in the outfield; and the picking-up and throwing-in are
magnificent, better than any I saw in New Zealand last year on holiday,
though it sounds absurd.

The story about the tree and fifty runs is two stories mixed up. They did
have to cut down a tree (inside the boundary), a sago palm too smooth to
climb. But it is a soft tree, like a banana, and the axe was got from a shed
and the tree down and the ball in to the wicketkeeper, before the batsman
had run six. (My sister and I – she scores, and is very keen – were sitting
under the tree, she was then new to things, and seeing a very excited
fieldsman dashing towards us and waving an axe, she resigned herself, I
think, to joining the noble army of martyrs.)

The 53 (not 59, let us be exact) was scored for a hit at Heuru, on San
Cristoval. I was umpire. We were playing on a sandy plateau twenty feet
above the beach, no boundaries. It was a fine hit to leg out to sea. The
weather had been terrible, and there was a tremendous surf tumbling in.
They wanted to call it a lost ball – the cowards – but I could see it, a nice
new red ball, bobbing about on the waves, and I said, 'Certainly not, run it
out.' Square-leg was a stumpy little chap, and they told him to go in; but he
looked at the surf thoughtfully. The team had to throw him in several
times before they got him out (he kept getting washed back). I was
wondering what to do about it. It was two o'clock, and we were to draw
stumps at sunset; but I am an ignorant umpire, and I couldn't remember
any cases of drawing stumps in the middle of a hit. However, I thought
after dark I can declare it a lost ball. Even so, how many runs are scored for
a ball lost after 600 runs have been run for a hit? However, it was all right,
they did get him out, and he swam to the ball. But it took a long time to

throw in. You know how it is when you are fielding in a very heavy sea, and how hard it is to throw far. The batsmen should have got more than 53, but they were very exhausted.

*The Cricketer Annual, 1931–32*

**Finally, a story of a man who collected bishops.**

# Religious Experience

One of the Norfolk Islanders was a real cricketer, a big man, over fifty when I knew him (but he played with the same zest till he was seventy). His great delight was bowling out bishops for ducks. He bowled a slow ball without break, but full of guile from change of pace, flight and length, and he 'created an atmosphere' (half the secret of a bowler), and studied every batsman, and tried various schemes to get him out. I fancy he had bowled out Bishop Patterson, he certainly had Bishop John Selwyn and Bishop Wilson for ducks. Later, the first game Bishop Wood played in, old Mauges bowled him for a duck. His last victim was Bishop Steward. By this time Mauges was nearly blind and could hardly see the batsman's wicket, but he sent down a straight one and got the Bishop first ball. He had also bowled the Bishop of Tasmania (on a visit) for a duck. So he realised his ambition, and still lives to dream happily of bishops and ducks.

By the way, did Bishop Molyneux tell you of the match between our XI, and a white XI, from the mission ship, *The Southern Cross?* For in that match he made top score for the whites. He made 1. John Tarani, our demon bowler, had just bowled the captain of the ship, middle stump. He felt he mustn't bowl the Bishop with the next ball, so he sent down a slow short one, which the Bishop hit for 1. I said, 'Tut! Tut! John,' and he showed no more misplaced pity. (The best thing in a glorious book I read the other day, the cricket memories of a Yorkshire parson, was a remark at the University match, 'Now, let's have none of that nonsense to-day about hoping the best team will win.')

*The Cricketer Annual, 1931–32*

We try to confine ourselves in these Far
Pavilion tales to countries and hinterlands
that do not enjoy Test status. But India
is so vast a country, and its cricket tra-
ditions so richly varied, that we feel
bound, in the Subcontinent's case, to
waive the rules. Indeed we start with a
veritable 'wrong un'.

# Who Invented the Googly?

This account of a cricket match more than a century ago
between the Bheel Corps and the Malegaon Cricket Club, in the
Khandeish District of the Bombay Presidency, must be one of the earliest
records, if not the very earliest, of a contest between an Indian and British
side.

The Bheels were a predatory tribe who for hundreds of years resisted
all attempts of the waves of conquerors from the North to subjugate them,
and the subsequent British efforts to tame them by force of arms met with
no better success. The tribesmen would lure their attackers into the
thousands of square miles of almost impenetrable jungle which they
inhabited and there, unheard and unseen, pick them off, one by one, with
poisoned arrows. It was not until the 1830s that James Outram, later of
Lucknow fame, obtained permission to recruit a para-military armed
force from the Bheels themselves on the poacher-turned-gamekeeper
principle, with the twin objects of suppressing dacoitry and of protecting
the villagers from the worst depredations of over-plentiful big game.

Outram's understanding of the Bheels and his almost legendary
reputation among them as a prince of hunters, together with the attrac-
tions of good quarters, food and pay and the opportunity to hunt with
firearms instead of spears and arrows, enabled him to enlist a *corps d'élite*
who were determined that if they themselves must forgo the pleasures of
dacoitry these should be denied to their fellow tribesmen too. The scheme
was an outstanding success, and in a few years their dense jungles became
as free from crime as any district in the Bombay Presidency.

When, in 1871, James Down, a 21-year-old Englishman, took up his
first police appointment in Khandeish, he became ex-officio adjutant to
the Bheel Corps and found to his surprise and delight that cricket was the
off-duty relaxation of all ranks. He was himself a keen cricketer and a
good bat, and nothing could have got him on good terms with his men
more quickly. This is how he described his cricketing experiences with
the Corps:

'In the evening cricket was the order of the day and made a strong appeal to the Bheels. As a cricketer from my early school days, I derived much pleasure and satisfaction from these games. The Bheels turned up in numbers and we used to pick sides daily, entering in a scorebook the names, runs made and other details in the approved manner. There was no slacking but all were on their toes, not content to wait for the ball in fielding but anticipating its direction and moving to meet it and covering much ground; they seldom let a ball pass and their catching and throwing were remarkably clean and accurate. I was not surprised at this for the Bheel is by nature keen, with splendid eyesight, agile as a cat and athletic in running, jumping and throwing, no doubt inherited from his wild life in the jungle where he survived by the accuracy of his shooting with bow and arrow and the use of his spear in hunting wild beasts.

'More remarkable, perhaps, than the fielding of the Bheels was their bowling, in particular that of Havildar (that is to say, sergeant) Khundoo and Sepoy Itoo. Both had acquired the knack of bowling with a break from the off to a remarkably consistent length, so that most balls pitched practically on the same spot, just clear of the off stump, with a break-back so as to take the leg stump. The spin was apparently imparted by a twist of the wrist rather than with the fingers. Both men took a very long run at speed before projecting the ball underarm at a great pace, but their approach to the wicket varied widely. Khundoo held the ball behind his back until he reached the wicket, when he would swing his arm round and hurl the ball with great force and remarkable accuracy. Itoo, on the other hand, would keep up a series of swinging movements of his arm round his back and head so that it was not easy to see at what exact moment the ball left his hands.

'Defence was alien to Bheel batting, nor did a straight bat appeal as the best way of getting runs, their sole objective. Thus they took the stance which they thought would best enable them to smite the ball for all they knew, quite irrespective of its length. So keen and alert was their sight that an innings would abound in huge hits with runs piled up in quick time, but the absence of accepted technique sooner rather than later brought with it its penalty and, as a rule, the innings could best be described as short and merry. Nevertheless, the bowling and fielding were so excellent as to more than counterbalance defective batting.

'It occurred to me that it would give a healthy stimulus to our cricket if I could arrange an "out" match with an eleven of Sahibs and provide our Bheels with a better idea of the generally accepted theory of batting as practised by English cricketers. Therefore, after obtaining the approval of my Superintendent, Major Olive Probyn, I challenged the Malegaon Cricket Club to take on my Bheels. I knew that this would be a good test as there was there a Native Regiment with a full complement of British officers as well as many civilians with some good cricketers who played in important matches such as the annual Presidency Match. Our challenge was accepted by the Club, which probably thought it would be amusing to play against the wild men of the jungle, however little this might provide in the way of serious cricket. I did not share their view, with my knowledge of the Bheels' prowess in the field, but in any event it could do them no harm to be beaten and pick up some idea of their limitations as batsmen.

'As the day of the great challenge match approached it was noticeable that the prospect gave a stimulus to the practice games as everyone hoped to be included in the eleven which was to battle for the honour of the Corps. The day before the match the selected team started out for Malegaon under the charge of Havildar Khundoo and next morning, before breakfast, Probyn (who was to act as one of the umpires) and I set off to ride the thirty miles there.

'Immediately after breakfast the match began. Having won the toss, I decided to bat first and to open the innings myself, feeling that the longer I could stay at the wicket the better I could control the impetuosity of my Bheels in this, their first match against an eleven of Sahibs. This precaution proved successful and I was able to carry my bat throughout the innings, scoring 71 out of a total of 140. This score fully realised my most sanguine hopes as the Bheels batted with greater restraint than I had anticipated and at no time got over-excited. So, when we went out to field to the bowling of Khundoo and Itoo, I had every hope that we were in sight of a win as this was the really strong department of our game. Nor was I disappointed; the bowling and fielding all round were really excellent with the result that we got our opponents out for 120-odd and thus won our first great match against a really good eleven of English cricketers by quite an easy margin.

'It was to me a real pleasure to see the tremendous enthusiasm of my Bheels when they realised that they had won, and not the least part of their rejoicings was that their Sahib had made a larger score than anyone on the other side. This loyalty to their leaders is an outstanding feature of the Bheel character and forms a strong link between officer and man in the Corps.'

So wrote James Down some fifty years later, drawing on his contemporary records and his own vivid memories of his early days in the Bombay police. There can be no doubt as to the general accuracy of his account, but if his detailed description of the bowling of Khundoo and Itoo is entirely accurate they must have been the inventors of the googly, though delivered underarm, and they must have attained a degree of accuracy never subsequently reached by their overarm successors from B. J. T. Bosanquet onwards. It is interesting to note some similarity in action between the 1971 Australian Test bowler Thomson and Itoo with the 'swinging movements of his arm round his back and head so that it was not easy to say at what exact moment the ball would leave his hand'. Finally, one wonders what would happen if Khundoo and Itoo could be resuscitated to play for India on the present tour!

NORMAN DOWN, *Spectator*, 26 June 1982

India again – this time in its Imperial
heyday.

# Cliff-hanging in the Raj

Situated as it is at a height of 6,300 feet, the playing field of
the Bishop Cotton School, Simla, must be one of the highest in the world.
It is true that there is one higher, at Goulmery in Kashmir, but that is not
in regular use, whilst the lovely grass cricket ground at Chail, the summer
headquarters of H.H. The Maharajah of Patiala, is about the same height.
His Highness blasted the top off a hill to create his ground, but those of us
with less ample means have to dig into the sides of our precipitous hills
and get a perch for house or ground, as the case may be, where we can.
Thus a ground 100 yards by 75, dug out of a hill in the Himalayas, is a
most rare and precious thing, and the school ground is the envy of many
cricketers in Simla, who are only too glad to take the opportunity of a game
on it. Of course, there are disadvantages. Without an ocean of water,
which is not available, it is impossible to keep grass on the field, and the
school, therefore, play on the hard earth, with bits of rock sticking through
in places to tear the fingers as one dives for the ball – in spite of this no one
wears gloves! – and the school's fielding, with brave use of the skies as a
second line of defence, is as smart as one could wish from a lot of active
young British boys. The pitch itself is of budgeree, covered with matting,
and the umpire is armed with a mallet to hammer back the stumps when
scattered.

The field is surrounded by wire supported on telegraph-posts fourteen
feet high, and 'sixes' are utterly discouraged. In ordinary games it is 'six
and out', followed by a tumble and scramble of 2,000 feet down into
Dhobi valley for the offender, whence he reappears an hour or so
afterwards, probably without the ball. In school matches six is awarded
only for straight drives over the bowler's head. Even then, and in spite of
small boys acting as gap-guards, it is no uncommon thing against some
visiting side with a good hitter to lose half a dozen balls in an afternoon.
Fortunately, Indian cricket balls are cheap (only the equivalent of 2s.), but
the bats suffer from the inevitable hardness of the balls, and a good
English bat rarely survives a good innings or two. In this respect we are
indeed between the devil and the deep sea, for whilst the English willow is
often too soft to stand up to the ball (apart from the prohibitive cost with
the import duty of $33\frac{1}{3}$ per cent), Indian willow is so heavy that it is
difficult to obtain a bat well-balanced and light enough for a boy. Still, the
game is played under difficult conditions, but with all the enthusiasm of
British boys for cricket all the world over, amidst mountains that dwarf the
mountains of Switzerland.

*The Cricketer Annual, 1929–30*

**In the thin air of the high mountains Tony Deane was press-ganged into playing with hill tribesmen in the Hindu Kush.**

# Cricket in the Hindu Kush

Overhead a falcon suddenly chattered in alarm as it quartered the bleak broken landscape. The utter silence was broken. At 10,000 feet in the foothills of the eastern Hindu Kush, loneliness and tranquillity frequently go hand in hand, and apart from the occasional glimpses of tribesmen hundreds of feet above me trekking into Afghanistan, I thought I was quite alone.

But the sense of isolation was breached by a familiar sound. The soft solid thud of ball hitting bat came through thin air. Looking at the hostile, rock-strewn countryside, relieved by the odd clump of rough spiky vegetation, I immediately diagnosed a dose of high altitude hallucinations. Again the sound reached me followed by cries of encouragement. Intrigued now and curious, I pinpointed the noise down the valley out of sight behind a sharp ridge. Following an animal track I walked down to the ridge and looked at the scene at my feet.

A group of local tribesmen, dressed in the pyjama-like garb of the North-West Frontier complete with a soft flat hat, were playing cricket on the only flat bit of ground I had seen in the mountains. Cleared of rocks about the size of golf balls, the ground scarcely accommodated the half-dozen or so fielders who, for obvious reasons, were guarding a boundary which marked the edge of a sharp drop into a stream some 2,000 feet below. A string of incomprehensible dialect sandwiched the universally recognized 'good shot' as the batsman sweetly cut the ball square from a delivery hurled down the pitch by an acrobatic bowler trailing yards of billowing cloth and leaving puffs of dust with every step.

For men used to playing a suicidal version of polo with a goat carcass, this must be an abject substitute. However, the sight of two armed tribesmen either side of the scorer seemed to sum up the seriousness of the game being played. Could vendettas include cricket matches, I asked myself?

There was a brief pause as I approached. A curious player came over.

'Salaam alikum,' I said in greeting.

'Alikum salaam,' he replied. 'Do you know this game?'

'Of course, my country invented it.'

'Are you real English?' (English-speaking *ferengi* are generally known as English whatever their nationality.)

I could see no possible danger in admitting I was a *real* English.

'You will play,' he said with just a hint of the interrogative. 'We stop when the sun goes down.' As this was in four hours' time, and I was still breathless from the walk down, I decided I didn't want to be cricket's first martyr buried in the eternal snows of the Hindu Kush. Anyway those armed spectators might not take too kindly to an infidel who dismissed their star player, whoever he might be.

Abdul whats-his-name swept another ball perilously close to the boundary of no return. The scorer entered a four next to a collection of hieroglyphics that could have been the local cure for diarrhoea. The next delivery vanished into the batsman's voluminous pantaloons, and a roar from the bowler suggested that anywhere else in the cricketing world, an appeal for leg before would have been just a formality. However, as there were no umpires, and a black look heavenwards elicited no help from Allah, the batsman stayed put.

Behind the bowler's arm the glittering 25,000-foot peak of Terrich Mir towered into a cerulean sky – an unbelievable sight-screen. Vast shadows crept across the valley, accentuating the deep defiles, as the sun moved westwards. Chukkor, a kind of mountain partridge, started calling high above us. A sudden crack echoed from hill to mountainside as an unseen marksman shot at something or other. A breath of icy wind reminded me it was time to climb back to my hut.

As the improbable scene disappeared behind the ridge, a muffled 'Howzat' proclaimed the possible end to Abdul I-never-learnt-the-rest-of-his-name's innings.

I pondered on the aerodynamics of a sphere of leather at 10,000 feet and felt I understood the Corinthian spirit at last.

TONY DEANE, *The Cricketer*, June 1985

**A surfeit of curry can often detract from the pleasure of touring India. Did this unlikely tale originate in the English dressing-room, we wonder?**

# That Curry Joke

A man goes into an Indian restaurant, and finds the menu confusing. There's a Taj Mahal curry, a Bombay curry, a Benares curry and many other variations. At the bottom of page 8, there's also a Boycott curry. He asks the waiter the difference between the various currys, to be told they are really pretty much the same.

'What's the Boycott curry then?' he asks.

'Oh sir, that's also almost the same as the others, but it takes longer to get the runs!'

JOHN LATIMER SMITH

> Burma is not a place to dally long in the
> outfield. If the leeches don't get you the
> Mustangs will.

# Burma Scars

One needed to keep very alert in the outfield in Moulmein in Burma. It was a remarkable setting, the pitch we had sorted out was surrounded by shrines. We played on grid netting that was used, more conventionally, as a take-off path for aircraft. We played with a tennis ball, hockey ball or whatever we could get hold of. The ball flew in all directions off the grid netting. This is what created the problem, for the outfield was inhabited by leeches and poisonous snakes so that quick eyesight and movement were essential qualities for the fielder.

Cricket in Burma proved most hazardous. At Bassein in South Burma, we were playing on an emergency landing strip. The teams were composed of RAF personnel and the Burmese groundstaff. Only four weeks previously, the area had been in the hands of the enemy. The news that it was now occupied by the Allies had obviously not reached one American pilot who came over in a Mustang and began shooting us up with his .5 inch guns! We all took successful evasive action but, in diving into the nearest brush, I was quite badly cut on some pineapple bushes which have leaves like swords.

CHRISTOPHER BOX-GRAINGER, taken from *A Walk to the Wicket*

> For the record, the Burma campaign was
> won by the British 14th Army, with just a
> little assistance from Errol Flynn and
> Meril's US Marauders. How suitable then
> that the victory should be celebrated with
> a game of cricket!

# In Darkest Burma

The end of the Japanese War found a Brigade of a famous Indian Division garrisoning, and attempting to maintain order, in the province of Tenasserim in darkest Burma. Here there is no real cold weather and the annual rainfall would submerge all but the mightiest of England's pavilions.

Cricket possibilities were small and we had practically no sports gear but we had two priceless assets – unlimited Jap labour, 19,000 to boot, and a very, very heavy roller. The choosing of a site for a wicket proved something of a problem as the only possible area in Thaton, where Brigade headquarters was situated, had already been purloined for a light aircraft landing strip. A compromise was finally achieved, twelve yards of flatish ground provided a net at Thaton and the Baluch Regiment, who had also won a roller, set about preparing a ground at Kyaikto, some forty miles north.

The Japs were mobilised and harnessed in incredible numbers to the roller. Others moved in an endless procession carrying empty petrol tins, which they filled with water at a stream, which ran a hundred yards or so from the net site, and deposited the accumulation of water on the pitch. Tent walls provided very adequate nets. The same scenes of furious activity raged at Kyaikto, the venue of the forthcoming contest on Sunday, 9 December.

Our equipment was like the curate's egg. The best features were one good Imperial Driver, with the handle bound by 4 × 2 (born 1936, still going strong), one box and The Cap. For balista we had one very whiskery cricket ball and two hockey balls. Pads were cunningly constructed by the farrier of a mule company using bamboo and saddle *numnahs*, batting gloves were non est – but we had one fine left-hand wicketkeeping glove. Bamboos were successfully fashioned into stumps and bails.

Practice was undertaken with a will and nets were held every evening from 4.30 to 6 p.m., when darkness stopped play. The Brigade Gurkha Defence Platoon provided the outfielders, their enthusiasm was unbounded and their determination to field the ball proved most alarming – a soccer tendency to head the ball or take a flying kick at it in mid-air being among the more disturbing features. A ball once retrieved was hurled at once with roars of laughter at either the luckless batsman or at the next bowler when about to deliver the ball. The wicket surprisingly proved to be an excellent one, it was crushed into submission, and all players survived safely for the great day, though three postings at the eleventh hour caused a final desperate search for substitutes.

Two days before the match a great coup was achieved – the purchase of three brand new cricket balls from far-off Rangoon. Here indeed was class, with a new ball for both innings and the doubtful hope, which was never realised, of one side scoring 200 runs and being able to demand the new ball.

On the fateful Sunday the team were early afoot and were safely ferried by the Japs across the Bilin River from where jeeps carried us to Kyaikto. No half-day cricket for us, this was the real thing with playing starting at eleven o'clock and continuing, if necessary, until darkness set in.

The Baluch had prepared a delightful ground, some even spoke in scorn of Canterbury. We had a pavilion; easy chairs under the shade of some adjoining trees; a scorer's box and two score-boards with telephonic communication to the scorers. Most important of all, there was plenty of gin and fresh limes. The only point on which we cavilled was the length of the boundaries, which were almost out of sight, and running between the wickets is no fun in Burma even in December. Runs would have been worth at least double on an ordinary ground.

The captains inspected the wicket, with professional thumb pressing. South of the Bilin won the toss and decided to bat. Our star, Mischler, of the Public Schools and Cambridge fame, who scored over 1,200 runs with an average of 87 for St Paul's in 1938, opened with easy elegance and was at once dropped at square-leg to be well caught there a few runs later. With our score standing at 47 for one, despite the disaster to our star, the opposition became distinctly worried.

It, however, proved unnecessary and lunch was insisted on with the very professional flourish of 97 for 9 – despite the fielding captain's assertion that it only required one more ball to complete our downfall. Perhaps our fall from grace was accelerated by the lordly manner in which our captain, who wore The Cap, insisted on the removal of a sleepy Pi Dog from behind the bowler's arm – this was regarded as unprecedented swank and galvanised the bowlers into furious and successful action.

An excellent lunch of cold bird and fruit salad sat very heavy on the visitors' tummies and they were thankful for the respite which the last pair provided by carrying the score to 109. North of the Bilin fared badly against Mischler's and Smeeton's fast swingers (or did rank and discipline help!) and lost five wickets for 11 runs. Hitting out masterfully they saved the follow-on and then proceeded to take six of their opponents' wickets for 10 runs, including that of Mischler for a duck. Having had a comfortable first innings lead of 63, but now only 73 on with but four wickets to fall, and with our bowlers nobbled by attentive waiters with double gins, South of the Bilin was definitely uneasy. However, our opponents flattered only to deceive and with the pitch showing signs of wear we ended up comfortable winners by 74 runs.

One final point must not go unmentioned, North of the Bilin's wicketkeeper had protected his most susceptible area with a cut-down Japanese fencing mask, worn outside the trousers, and early on a bull'seye rang its vindication over the field.

BRIGADIER G. P. L. WESTON, *The Cricketer Spring Annual, 1946*


Cricket in Singapore is more than just a
game for mad dogs and Englishmen, as
Rowland Bowen reveals.

# Gamblers

There is much competitive inter-state cricket: Singapore – an Independent State now – has its own strong team too, but still no stronger than one of the better-equipped Malay States. Cricket is played in the schools, and it is popular amongst almost all the non-indigenous and Chinese population. Whether it will ever 'take' with the Malays or the Chinese generally is an open question: that the Chinese are interested is obvious to anyone who has seen the Chinese crowds around a match there. Though a question would arise in the onlooker's mind: just what were they doing, because most of them seemed to have their backs to the game? The answer is that the Chinese in those parts are quite inveterate gamblers, and have found cricket an unsurpassed medium for betting: whether a named batsman would score any runs off the fourth ball of the over, and if so how many – and so on. Just as in England football pools have perpetuated an interest in soccer which might well otherwise have dwindled, it could be that in Malaysia and Singapore gambling will eventually cause the Chinese to take part more actively in the game.

ROWLAND BOWEN, *Cricket: a History of its Growth and Development throughout the World*

**Has this ever happened at Lord's? A tale of murder from the Indian Ocean.**

# An Arrested Batting Talent

When I played in Asmara the pitch had been marked out on a parade ground which was all that was available to us. On some of the islands in the Indian Ocean on which I played conditions were quite favourable, but the games sometimes bizarre. I was concerned with RAF Communications and was operating in the Indian Ocean. Several of the islands were, in fact, prison islands, and on one of them, in the Andaman group, I was engaged in a match which was being played with the utmost charm and good manners. My opening partner was a particularly charming and modest man who was batting quite beautifully. He had reached 49 not out and I was at the bowler's end when four armed policemen marched on to the field. The sergeant addressed me politely, but firmly, 'I am sorry, tuan, but the game must not go on.' When I enquired why we had to stop, he and his men marched to the other end of the wicket where he arrested my partner (49 not out) on a charge of multiple murder. He had evidently been on parole when he committed the crime, his guilt being proved conclusively a week later.

CHRISTOPHER BOX-GRAINGER, taken from *A Walk to the Wicket*

E. W. Swanton compares this tragic tale to
the Munich Air Disaster. May we not suggest that its impact was even greater, because it affected a very small European
population surrounded by natives?

## Hong Kong Shipwreck

An episode in Hong Kong's history is one of the most
dramatic in the history of cricket. Seventy years ago an entire representative team was lost. There has been nothing comparable in sporting
records, the nearest probably being the air crash at Munich killing a
number of the Manchester United Football team.

Hong Kong Cricket Club, now in its 114th year, had formed the
enterprising habit of having a fixture with Shanghai Cricket Club, 800
miles to the north. Indeed the length of time Hong Kong has been touring
overseas is a distinctive feature in its history, for 98 years ago Hong Kong
first travelled to Shanghai in return for Shanghai's first visit the year
before.

These efforts were apparently too exhaustive. It was twenty-two years
before this remarkable series of inter-port fixtures was resumed. Soon
afterwards, in 1882, one of the best all-rounders in the Army stationed in
Hong Kong, Captain J. Dunn, who had scored nearly 3,000 runs in a
previous season, was the captain of the team of thirteen touring Shanghai.
After having been seen off by their hosts, the Hong Kong team on the
P & O steamer *Bokhara* ran quickly into a typhoon. Mountainous seas
rolled over the ship, extinguishing the engine-room fires; without power
the ship drifted towards the Pescadores Archipelago near Formosa and on
to the deserted Sand Island. It struck at midnight, sinking immediately. A
total of 125 were drowned, all except twenty-one personnel and two
passengers; these were two of the team.

E. W. SWANTON, *The World of Cricket*

The problems of finding decent opposition in China, the perils of travel having
just been highlighted, explain the failure
of cricket to take hold of the populace. It
remained very much an ex-pat affair.

## The Race Course at Tsing Tao

The actual first game ever to be played at Tsing Tao was
played last week v. HMS *Medway* on the Chinese Stadium, but ours was
the first match on their own ground on the race course.

It is more or less public ground, and is bordered by the race course to
the westward, the golf course to the eastward, the hockey and baseball
grounds to the southward, and rough ground to the northward. These
comprise the boundaries, and incidentally, a couple of basketball goals
had to be dug up and removed before we started to play. The outfield was
decidedly on the rough side, which made ground fielding a little difficult –
the pitch itself being a matting wicket laid on to a prepared strip. Possibly,
a fast bowler might have been dangerous on this wicket, but neither side
had one to call upon, and so one can only conjecture upon the result if we
had had a Larwood playing. But the pitch was certainly 'interesting'
enough to make batting an art of concentration in watching the ball closely
– as shown by the score-board.

Tsing Tao won the toss and decided to bat first. Helped by moderately
good bowling and keen fielding, but much more so by the intricacies of the
pitch, we managed to dismiss our opponents for 17 runs. HMS *Eagle* did
not fare very much better, for after our first-wicket pair had passed our
opponents' total, a collapse followed and we were all out for 41.

After an enormous tea, supplied very kindly by the English ladies of
Tsing Tao, our opponents went in to bat again, and one of the most
amazing collapses I have ever seen took place. They actually started very
promisingly, having 42 runs on the board for four wickets; but were all out
for 43. I put A. B. Clements on to bowl when the total was 42, and he took
a wicket with his first ball, and followed this by the 'hat-trick' with his last
three balls.

The bowler at the other end continued the good work by taking two
wickets with his first two balls, and very nearly had the batsman stumped
with his third ball for another 'hat-trick'. No further runs were scored this
over, and so in two overs, six wickets had fallen for 0 runs – and five
wickets to consecutive balls. In Able-Seaman Clements' second over, he
had a single scored off his first ball, and then clean bowled the last man,
his final analysis reading:

| Overs | Maidens | Runs | Wickets | Average |
|-------|---------|------|---------|---------|
| 1.2   | 1       | 1    | 5       | 0.2     |

We lost two wickets in getting the necessary 18 runs to win, which we managed to do at 6.28 – the time for drawing stumps being 6.30.

It was a wonderfully amusing and interesting afternoon's cricket, and everyone thoroughly enjoyed it. The keenness and enthusiasm shown by the local inhabitants was a joy to watch, and their hospitality to us was marvellous. I think there is no doubt that cricket has come to stay here, and with their great enthusiasm they will develop into a very good side – the only difficulty at present being that you cannot prevent the local golfing enthusiasts from practising their shots to within twenty yards of the pitch, and also on race days from preventing any Tom, Dick and Harry watching the races from the pitch itself.

LIEUT.-COMMANDER F. M. R. STEPHENSON,
*The Cricketer Spring Annual, 1935*

**When the Chinese did play, their approach was inventive, to say the least. We have here the first and perhaps the last attempt to make cricket a labour-saving activity. Certainly it did not catch on in Shanghai.**

## Labour Saving Cricket

The Chinese themselves did not take readily to cricket and when they announced their intention of giving an exhibition of the game near Shanghai many of the English residents were much interested. 'When the game began all the fielders were gathered together in a bunch and the gabble was deafening. When the bowler bowled it was noticed that a long string was attached to the ball and the other end was secured to the bowler's thumb. Of course the ball could only traverse the length of the string, thereby avoiding the necessity of any long fielders and only two runs in all the play were accomplished. The English laughter became unlimited – but the poor Chinese looked much abashed and foolish for they evidently expected to be praised for the ingenuity in saving bodily exertion.'

*The Cricketer Annual, 1922–23*

'In July or August of 1952,' a puzzled correspondent writes, 'a letter to *The Times* reported a consignment of 147 bats arriving in Tibet. This bizarre item of information has haunted me ever since. Who plays cricket in Tibet? Can you throw any light on the problem?' Recourse to *The Times* is our only answer . . .

# Bats to Tibet

Neither the Foreign Office nor the MCC has seen fit to comment on a report from Kalimpong that a large consignment of cricket bats, transported on the backs of mules, is on its way to Lhasa at the behest of the education authorities in Tibet. Accustomed as we are to being baffled by international affairs, it is difficult to recall any recent development in that sphere of which the significance was harder to evaluate. There is, of course, nothing odd in the Tibetans wanting to play cricket; this natural and salutary aspiration does them credit. The mountain torrents of their native land and her frequently frozen lakes severely limit the opportunities open to wet-bobs, and it was perhaps inevitable that a passion for our national sport, repressed for centuries, should break out sooner or later.

It is, all the same, a little surprising that King Willow should come into his own at a time when Tibet is under Communist control. It may, of course, be that the new regime in Lhasa sees in cricket an opiate or anodyne which will confer upon the people partial oblivion of their sufferings; and it is certainly true that the history of the game is unsullied by any connexion with counter-revolutionary activity. But there are, after all, other sports less closely associated with the Imperialist tradition; and, however much one reveres cricket and however little one knows about Tibet, it is difficult to believe that this incomparable game is ideally suited to the conditions obtaining on the Roof of the World.

There may – indeed there must – be more in this business than meets the eye. It looks like some sort of a move in the Cold War. Readers with romantic minds will toy with the idea that the whole thing has been organised, for subversive purposes – by the British Secret Service – that at the head of the caravan (humming the Eton boating song to put people off the scent) strides, heavily disguised, some agent of the calibre of Colonel Egham or Big White Carstairs. Alas, it is more likely to be the other way round. World Communism, though it has many conquests to its credit, has as yet made little impression on cricket; but its outward indifference to the sport (the Russians have not even bothered to claim that they invented it) may well mask a respect for its civilising influence and a determination to adapt it to conform with the exigencies of Marxist doctrine. It is true that Tibet does not seem a particularly sensible place in which to initiate this project; but it is remote and secluded, and the inhabitants have no preconceived bourgeois ideas on the subject which need to be eradicated. It seems all too probable that the report from Kalimpong may foreshadow the launching of a vast conspiracy throughout the New Democracies to undermine the influence of cricket by evolving a similar but ideologically sounder game. How fast or how far this threat to one of our dearest institutions may develop it is impossible to say. It depends, to a certain extent, on whether the people in Lhasa remembered to order any balls.

'Fourth leader' in *The Times*, 1952
(brought to our attention by Olive Clarke)

Twenty-five years later David Rayvern Allen reported a game he saw in Tibet played by Tibetans. Perhaps *The Times*'s prophecy is coming true.

## Playing Chokchokpa in Tibet

The ground was rough – and the ball blue. Yes, a blue ball in terrain that is now an extension of the Red Flag. I had thought that there was only one blue ball extant. Surely they hadn't borrowed it? After all, it was rumoured that some of the playing utensils as well as limited tuition had filtered through Northern India. Imagine calling the curator at Lord's:
'Is the ball still there?'
'Which one?'
'The blue one.'
'We don't have blue balls.'
Relieved to hear it but –
'– it's the ladies' one –'
Surely he'd remember the ladies' ball? It was there for all to see – a cosseted inmate of the Long Room.
'– it was in the 1890s actually, you know, the firm of Alfred Reader manufactured –' a singular relic to prevent the stronger sex swooning at the sight of a rubicund projectile.

DAVID RAYVERN ALLEN, *The Cricketer*, April 1977

An innocent comment from James
Shepherd to the Director of the Korea
Trade Centre landed him in hot water. If
he is correct it may land *us* in trouble by
1996.

# Exporting Cricket to Korea

It all began when I was having lunch with the Director of the
Korea Trade Centre, one bleak December day in London. The small
publishing company that I run did a certain amount of work for South
Korea, and the Director and I were discussing ways of improving relations
between English and South Korean businessmen.

As a result of the excess amount of wine that I drink on these occasions I
rashly asserted that the Koreans could never understand the English
mentality until they knew something about cricket. Why do we say, for
example, 'It is not cricket'? Why not 'It is not football', or any other game
you care to name? Why 'playing a straight bat' or 'I am stumped for an
answer'? And what are foreigners – particularly those nine thousand miles
away in North-east Asia – to make of 'batting on a sticky wicket'? After all,
did not Neville Cardus say that 'cricket somehow holds up the mirror to
the English nature'? And what more quintessentially English occasion
could there be than a game of cricket on a hot, drowsy summer's afternoon
on a ground encircled by trees and perhaps overlooked by a church, 'As
the run-stealers flicker to and fro' – the unique sound of bat on ball, the
smell of new-mown grass, the floral-hatted ladies, tea in the pavilion, and
so on and so on?

Aware of my host's uncomprehending stare, I sought help from yet
another glass of Pouilly Fumé and went on to suggest that, for the price of
yet another good lunch, I would be happy to give the staff of the Korea
Trade Centre an hour's lecture on cricket – its rules (very briefly), its
history and the way the game has moulded English character and culture –
followed by half an hour's questions.

To my horror, the Director thought it a splendid idea, and promised to
make arrangements for such a lecture to take place the following month.

On the way back to the office I thought no more about the subject. After
all, in my dealings with diplomats and other high-ranking officials from
the Far East I found that a decision on any undertaking would take them
six months or a year of consultation among themselves, and then the
project would take just as long to work its way up through the layers of
Asian bureaucracy. Minutes would be made at meetings and the 'Action'
columns filled with Korean names difficult for Western tongues but
which, when translated into *Hangul*, the Korean language, mean 'tiger on
a rock' or 'sword of gold'. At follow-up meetings the response to 'What
progress did you make on this, Mr Kim/Park/Lee?' would be a quizzical

gaze. How on earth did they beat us at shipbuilding (amongst much else)? Of course, once a decision was made, you had to move like lightning.

The telephone was ringing as I entered the office, and it was not the Director of the Trade Centre but the Press and Cultural Attaché of the Embassy of the Republic of Korea.

'Mr Shefferd (always problems with pronouncing my name). Ambassador would like you to give lecture on cricket to Embassy staff.'

Now I knew how Stan McCabe felt, in the first Test at Sydney in 1932, when told he was next in to face Larwood. Brave front. Look how he performed that day!

'Delighted, Mr Kim/Park/Lee. When?'

I hoped for a few weeks' grace. I *could* produce something at short notice and had, after all, played an inordinate amount of cricket in my youth, much more than was good for my academic record, believing that to know by heart who opened the batting and bowling for every English county side in the 1950s was much more important than, say, learning about the Reform Bill of 1832. I still do, in a way. And I had played cricket for my college at university – an opening batsman in the (later) Boycott mould, sometimes accelerating to 10 runs an hour, and a bowler in the Maurice Tate style, hoping that any increase in the pace of the ball off the pitch would make up for what I could not put into the initial delivery.

'Next week,' came the reply, and my heart sank.

Still, I knew the rules of the game and the Koreans would not, I prayed, know the first thing about cricket. So, to mix games, advantage to me. But the history? Cricket has always been there, hasn't it? I knew about two-stump wickets, underarm bowling and bats shaped like hockey-sticks in the eighteenth and nineteenth centuries, but what about the medieval period and earlier? And how on earth *did* it mould English character? And what time did the public library close, so that I could dash round and take out an armful of books on the history of the game?

Baseball! The Koreans, heavily influenced by the Americans in their troubled past forty years, play the game with great enthusiasm. If I could take baseball as a reference point and show how cricket differed, I had some kind of a start.

So – rules, history, character and culture were cobbled together into sketchy notes by the following weekend, but I needed 'props', cricket gear that my audience could handle (I was by now becoming quite enthusiastic about the whole thing). Let them feel a cricket ball to see how hard it is (tell them how it is made), say that it is no joke to have this object bowled (thrown) at you from just 20 yards (translate into metres) away, travelling at over 90 miles (translate it into kilometres) an hour. Let them swing the bat – wood from the willow only, bamboo handle (they grow bamboo in Korea) with rubber splices. Let them try on pads and gloves and emphasise how *dangerous* a game cricket is.

So, on another wintry day, a week later, I arrived by taxi at the Korean Embassy in Kensington with cricket gear, kindly lent by a friend at King's College, London, tumbling out of a splitting bag, and overtipped a bemused taxi-driver. I strode into the Embassy's large reception room, leaving a trail of bails, stumps, balls and gloves behind me as I went to meet my audience and, I felt, my Maker. McCabe had it easy compared with this.

Twenty or so impassive Oriental faces followed my progress to the lectern and then that of one of the balls as it rolled to the back of the room. The Ambassador's chauffeur stood by the blackboard, ready with cleaning cloth. And in the front row sat the Ambassador, the Chargé d'Affaires and their aides, the highest-ranking South Koreans in Britain, ready to be initiated into a national religion that makes the rites of shamanism look very straightforward, commonplace events.

Language, of course, would be a problem. These diplomats had a much greater command of English than most of their fellow-countrymen back in the Korean peninsula, but what were they to make of some of the arcane terms used in cricket? For us, a cricket ball never bounces, it pitches. What are they to make of a ball that breaks? And silly point, short fine leg? O God, 'O my Hornby and my Barlow long ago'!

I took off my watch and placed it beside my notes, as if this was something I did every day of the week, and began with a quotation from the Research Organisation Political and Economic Planning 1956 Report, which is worth repeating here:

> What is cricket? It is a peculiarly English game: not suitable for export and found only in places where Englishmen have taken it. Cricket is an expression of the English character and, as such, is inscrutable.

I looked up from my notes and found that reaction to this was, also, inscrutable. So, after a brief exposition of the objectives of cricket and the points of departure from those of baseball (What *are* the rules of baseball? ... I knew how to play rounders), I passed the cricket gear among the audience and turned to the blackboard to draw field-placings for a typical opening of an innings. To add drama, I drew a very attacking 'umbrella' field – Jardine's leg-theory had nothing on this – and put the captain – virtually the only man in front of the wicket – at mid-off. I explained why a match always begins with fast bowlers (pitchers), how the seam affects the flight of the ball, why it is so important for the ball to keep its shine and why players do this by polishing it on their trousers. (A look on the nodding face of one of the audience indicated that, at last, he realised that this was not some ritualistic gesture akin to casting a voodoo spell but merely the cause of a substantial laundry bill.)

All was going well until I introduced the batsmen, a striker and a non-striker. Hand raised.

'Why is there a non-striker?'

'Because after an over (six balls) is bowled (thrown), the fielders (catchers) change ends (sides of the field) and the striker at one end becomes the non-striker.' Hand raised.

'Why?'

'Because a cricket team comprises eleven players, loses ten wickets (strikers) and there is always a player not out (still playing).' Hand raised.

'Why is one batsman still playing?'

'Then (ignoring this last question) when a side (team) is out the other side goes in until they are out and then, in a county or Test match, the other side goes in until they are out.' (There is, I think a printed tea-towel that explains the rules much more clearly than I did that day.)

Thankfully, I passed on to the game's history. Stoolball, trapball, tipcat, cat and dog – all those medieval (and earlier) ancestors of cricket appeared on and vanished from the blackboard. On to the 1700s, with the game being taken up by an aristocracy deprived of its military power by the state and given vast tracts of land where they could play these games as mock duels. My audience became perceptibly more attentive when I emphasised the democratic influence of cricket in those times, when the greatest duke had to mix with the humblest on his estate, face the fastest (underarm) balls from his local blacksmith and accept a dubious decision from one of his gardeners, acting as umpire. We think of England as a class-ridden society but in Korea it is almost more so, with just two strata – the elite (well educated, well off) and the rest.

On to the changing shape of stumps and bat, the adoption of the game by the middle classes, Hambledon, MCC, Lord's, from under- to round- to overarm bowling, losing the 'Ashes' in 1882 (good story there about the burning of the bails – another pagan ritual?), cricket exported to all parts of the British Empire, and so on up to the present. As I spoke, I noticed with foreboding that all this was being quietly absorbed by my audience, an expression of rapt concentration on their faces. As we have discovered to our cost, the Far East learns fast. A national Korean cricket team in 1996? Another 'Ashes' fiasco two years later, with perhaps my own ashes – the result of action by a vengeful English cricket community – in a beautiful Koryo-period celadon pot?

The final section on English character went down best. The English love of the countryside, love of order, team spirit, the game's ruthlessness – one mistake and you are usually out (bring in the Falklands War; bring in the English demand for unconditional surrender by the Germans in the Second World War) – all these aspects set my audience commenting among themselves.

The question session, which I had dreaded, presented no great problems.

'Does the ball have to bounce?' came from the back of the room.

'No, but that is what we call a full toss, and it is a *bad* ball because it can be hit for six. You will remember that I explained a six-hit earlier.' Then followed five minutes on the advantages of making the ball pitch (bounce).

The total scores after five days (*five days!*) of a Test created a problem bordering on the metaphysical. After all, if England score 200 all out in the first innings (session), Australia 300 in their first innings, England 400 in their second, and Australia 250 for 5 wickets (strikers) and then run out of time, then surely England, with more runs, have won? Hand raised.

'A draw? Why?' Why, indeed.

Stumps were laid, with bails on top, against a wall. I took the bat, and a colleague – a legendary leg-break bowler in his time – the ball, and he mimed leg-breaks, off-breaks, top-spin, cutters, inswing and outswing, while I despatched them all with ease to an imaginary boundary. What would passers-by have thought if they had seen a cricket ball rocketing through the Embassy windows? And what if Buckingham Palace had telephoned, only to be told that his Excellency the Ambassador for the Republic of Korea at the Court of St James was being shown how to bowl a googly? The mind boggles.

I received, if not a standing ovation, then warm applause – and that lunch. A repeat performance at the Trade Centre followed a month later, but now I had my notes and took it all into my stride. Now, as the staff changes, I am asked to lecture once a year at the Korean Embassy, and it even makes the Korean newspapers (in the 'Events' column). Korean friends now attend Test matches and give me their highly informed opinions on the day's play.

But I am still filled with foreboding about the possible outcome of all this exporting of cricket to Korea, and I am not looking forward to 1996. Look what they did to us in the area of shipbuilding (and much else).

JAMES SHEPHERD

The inspiration behind our Japanese tales was a comment from Nigel Hoygarth, Chairman of the Cricket Society. Looking at the picture on the cover of *Tales From Far Pavilions* with its geisha girls and pagodas, he enquired why we had no Japanese tales. He then promptly started us off with a number of clippings of his own. The first was an encouraging little note from Professor Yamada Makoto.

## 'Cricket is Going Great'

'I have good news of cricket in Japan on 1983's season. Cricket is going great in Kobe and Yokohoma, Japan.

We had net practice, and very exciting and wonderful matches from June to November.

Before 1984's season I establish JAPAN CRICKET ASSOCIATION in co-operation with many international cricketers, English Australia, Indian, who lives in Japan.

Yours sincerely,

Makoto Yamada

Letter to The Cricket Society, 24 December 1983

Mr Hoygarth also highlighted the missionary activity of one Danyll Wills and provided this report from the pages of *The Times*.

## Letter from Kyoto

Both the Emperor Meiji and the Marylebone Cricket Club would be surprised by a scene that will be played out in western Japan this weekend. Six young Japanese will be playing a trial match to decide who will represent Kobe port in a series of cricket matches against the port of Yokohama. It seems likely that most, if not all, the six will make the mixed team of Japanese and foreigners who will be reviving the inter-port game. Cricket has been played in Japan since the 1860s.

In that time, however, few Japanese have taken to the game and the contests have usually been between teams of resident foreigners, or against teams from visiting warships and the like.

This time, however, thanks to the enthusiasm of a young Englishman distressed at the Japanese predilection for the barbarian alternative, baseball, the six will probably give a good account of themselves.

All the players, says Mr Danyll Wills, their Cambridge coach, are 'very good' and would make useful additions to any university side in Britain.

Mr Wills, who teaches at Kobe University of Foreign Studies, has brought most of them to the game by his lucid and attractive description of its intellectual and tactical aspects. The Japanese, he feels, would have made good players of the game, with its equal demands on brawn and brain, had the Americans not arrived first.

Mr Wills, with his huge mutton-chop whiskers and metal-rimmed glasses, looks not unlike the first foreigners whom the Emperor Meiji encouraged to visit Japan. But even the Emperor, like most Japanese, would have been discouraged to learn the weight of the ball, and the speed of its delivery.

The six players, however, and Professor Makoto Yamada of the university, have overcome their fears and practise regularly together twice a week. The 'season' begins about now, both because the weather in Japan is more temperate, and because it fits in with university activities. It ends about New Year, and resumes again in April.

'All those who have tried have liked it,' Mr Wills said. 'I find that, if you can break the first barrier, people like it. After all, everyone here enjoys hitting a ball.'

Not all their matches have been easy. A recent game in the ancient capital of Nara came close to being a serious loss of face for the intrepid cricketers, who usually manage to turn out in something approaching whites.

It was supposed to be a demonstration match, with the visitors showing the Nara neophytes how it was done. But the captain disgraced himself, and it looked as though there was going to be a disaster – much to the delight of the Nara players, who had never hit a ball in earnest before – until Kobe's Japanese answer to Colin Cowdrey saved the day.

Not surprisingly, the Japanese game has given rise to a whole new series of descriptive expressions, which make John Arlott sound positively boring. There is the Geisha Glance, the Kamikaze Cut, the Yokohama Yorker, not to mention the Hara-kiri Hook.

Such levity, however, detracts from the truly serious nature of Mr Wills' real ambition. Being at heart a China specialist, he wants eventually to coach a Chinese team, and stage matches between Japan and China.

He believes that the Chinese would ultimately triumph. But he could be wrong. Japan is, after all, the only country in the world with a cricket ball at the centre of its flag.

DAVID WATTS, *The Times*, 9 October 1982

As is probably clear by now the two cen-
tres for cricket in Japan are Kobe and
Yokohoma. Both are ports and both had a
Royal Naval presence.
The first reported game was in 1865
when the Fleet played Kobe. Such was the
political situation at the time that the
players wore side arms!
J. A. Dean describes the situation in the
early 1920s.

# The Rising Sun v. The Rest

There are only two clubs in Japan where the game is played,
namely, the Kobe Cricket Club and the Yokohama Country and Athletic
Club (YC & AC). As these clubs are over four hundred miles distant from
each other, it is only possible to arrange a game between them once a year.
For the rest of the season pick-up games are played each weekend. Seeing
that there are no other sides to play against, it is rather wonderful that
interest in the game is maintained, and in the very hot summer months,
with the temperature at 90 degrees, it is not always easy to raise two
elevens to play each other. The counter-attractions of bathing and
week-ending in the lovely Japanese country are very strong.

The wicket used is matting over grass. Very little grass is grown in
Japan, and most of it is bamboo grass, which is most unsuitable for cricket.
Two pieces of matting are used, each stretched from the middle of the
pitch as far as the popping crease, and you make your block up against the
edge of the matting. The two pieces of matting are tied together in the
middle, and should a ball bowled hit this join in the matting it is treated as
an 'undelivered ball', and does not count in the over or in the score. The
pitch generally plays excellently, and it is very seldom indeed that an
untrue bounce is noticed.

The players are almost all Britishers; no Japanese play the game, and
very few of them understand it at all.

The season is from May till the first week in October. In Kobe the only
available ground is owned jointly by the Japanese and the foreigners, and
as the Japanese have the use of it each Sunday, cricket can only be placed
on Saturdays. At Yokohama the YC & AC own their ground, and cricket is
played alternately on Saturdays and Sundays, the Americans using it for
baseball similarly. Throughout the season nets are up on Tuesdays and
Thursdays, and quite a few enthusiasts leave their offices in Tokyo and
make the journey of an hour and a half to the ground to get a 'net' of some
fifteen minutes.

In Kobe this year the staff of the 'Rising Sun' (Asiatic Petroleum Co.)
were able to raise a team and challenge the Rest, though they met with
defeat, and in Yokohama in 1926 an Insurance XI also went down to

defeat against the Rest. For the rest the games are Over 30 v. Under 30, Married v. Single, Frothblowers v. Non-Frothblowers. Sometimes a game is played against a 'P and O' or Blue Funnel steamer in port, though naturally this opposition is not strong.

Last year Yokohama were fortunate in having the assistance of Hon. D. F. Brand, who was with A. C. MacLaren's team in New Zealand, and Capt. K. S. Himatsinhji, a brother of the famous K. S. Duleepsinhji. Both these players turned out for the game against Kobe, and yet Yokohama lost by an innings and over 100 runs!

These Interport games date back to 1884, and each year are looked forward to with great interest. With the earthquake of 1923 Yokohama were badly hit, and it was with difficulty that a side was raised in 1924, and they have not won a game since. But the tide will turn, and as Kobe have only won fifteen games against Yokohama's twenty-five (three drawn) they have some way to go to get level. In Yokohama the Interports are three-day affairs and in Kobe only two days, owing to the ground not being available on a Sunday.

J. A. DEAN, *The Cricketer Spring Annual, 1928*

An ugly diplomatic incident blew up in 1909 about the site of the Yokohama Cricket Ground. It became a matter for concern for Her Majesty's Britannic Government.

# The Case of the Yokohama Cricket Ground

During the past year an acute difference of opinion took place between a militant section of the Yokohama community and His Majesty's consul-general on the one side and his Excellency Governor Sufu and the local Government on the other. The case has given rise to a vast amount of correspondence and a considerable amount of bad feeling. The embassy was appealed to and eventually the question in dispute was referred to His Majesty's Secretary of State.

The dispute arose over a very handsome piece of turf some 5,516 tsubo, or just over four and a half acres in extent, which formed the centre and rather more than a fourth of the so-called public garden of Yokohama. This piece of turf was enclosed within a high paling, and was leased to the members of an institution called the Yokohama Cricket and Athletic Club, entirely composed of foreigners, three-quarters British.

Briefly, the history of the public garden and that part of it called the cricket ground (though used for football, baseball, and other games) is as follows:

The port of Yokohama was opened in 1859; on 19 December 1864, a convention, relating to improvements and public works in the foreign settlement, was concluded between the Japanese Government and the consular body. Among other matters it was provided that a certain piece of ground should be reserved for the purposes of recreation.

In 1884 the present Yokohama Cricket and Athletic Club came into existence, and an arrangement was made with the authorities for an extension of the area of the pitch, and an agreement was signed in the form of a temporary lease whereby the club had exclusive control of the ground on payment to the governor and city authorities of a fixed rental.

In 1899, after the revision of the treaties, the 1884 agreement was cancelled, and a lease was drawn up for ten years, expiring in 1909.

In July 1907 the present governor of Kanagawa Ken, Baron Sufu, gave warning to the president and committee of the club that 'the lease would not be renewed on any conditions whatsoever at its expiry in 1909,' and this decision was made emphatic both verbally and in writing. The president and committee approached me on the subject and in a written statement begging me to use my influence with the governor to obtain a renewal of the lease, they state the probable reasons which actuated the governor in refusing to grant a renewal of the lease. 'When the privilege of exclusively using a part of the public garden was first granted to the Yokohama Cricket and Athletic Club, and for many years afterwards, the Japanese population of Yokohama was comparatively small, and did not appreciate the privilege of a public garden as they have learned to do recently. The cricket ground occupies the centre of the oblong area constituting the public garden, so that from whatever point it is entered the visitor soon perceives the fence enclosing a well-kept and tempting square of verdure, reserved for the use of foreigners. It is not surprising that a reservation so prominently placed meets with the disapproval of some of the citizens, natives of the land, and such people have no doubt made representation to the authorities.' In the course of representations which I subsequently made to the governor and also the central authorities, I ascertained that at one time a notice was placed on the palings to the effect that no Japanese were allowed to enter the 'tempting square of verdure'; this notice was bitterly resented, and with considerable reason, by the 'natives of the land', and doubtless accounted for a good deal of the unsympathetic manner in which a request for the renewal of the lease was treated by the authorities. It is to be noted that even now no Japanese can be members of the Yokohama Cricket and Athletic Club.

No particular notice was taken at the time of the governor's refusal to renew the lease. On 29 July 1909, the lease expired, but the governor extended the period until 29 October of the same year, but gave notice that the club fixtures, pavilion, palings, etc. must be removed by that date. Against this notice the committee, acting under the advice of the British consul-general and conjointly with him, lodged a protest with the governor, raising for the first time the point that foreigners had a treaty right in conjunction with Japanese to play cricket and take other forms of exercise on that particular piece of verdure called the cricket ground. The governor, in the meanwhile, had suggested a compromise, and had proposed setting apart a portion of the public garden more on one side and transferring thereto the club's turf, etc., and this proposal had been practically accepted by the embassy in a semi-official note to the Japanese Foreign Office; the official pointed out, however, that he could take no steps to carry out his proposal until and unless the protest which had been made to him was withdrawn. Acting under the influence and advice of the consul-general, and supported by a meeting of the younger members of the club, the committee declined to withdraw the protest. Subsequently, saner counsels prevailed and by a large majority it was decided to do so, and the protest was subsequently withdrawn. The present condition of the case is that the cricket ground is to be transferred to another part of the public garden; the regulations regarding the same will doubtless not be of so exclusive a character, so far as the Japanese are concerned.

This case acquired an importance, and wasted an amount of time and energy, quite out of all proportion to its merits, due almost entirely to the attitude taken by the British consul-general and his small but noisy following.

The matter, at the earnest request of the citizens of Yokohama, was eventually referred to the Foreign Office, and in a despatch dated 7 December 1909, the Secretary of State gave it as his opinion that 'if the Japanese authorities think that it is now desirable to relegate the games to a different portion of the gardens, I am not of opinion that His Majesty's Government can object on the score of treaty rights.' This was the view this embassy had taken of the case from the commencement. The Secretary of State further said that 'with regard to the attitude of the Japanese authorities nothing would seem to show that they have any intention or any desire to be unreasonable or of not carrying out their obligations.'

During the past year the Japanese authorities, that is, the governor of the province and the mayor of Yokohama, have shown every desire to carry out their obligations; cricket, football, and baseball have in their appointed season been played upon the old ground until the last moment possible; the turf comprising the cricket pitch has been carefully and skilfully removed to the new ground, and it is hoped that cricket will be commenced as soon as the season opens.

*Annual Report on Japan for the Year 1910*

To finish, a report from the Kobe Regatta
and Athletic Club Magazine.

# Hello Ladies!

Cricket is going great at Isogami Ground but there are not sufficient KR & AC members playing, probably because many are away on holiday. As per schedule, we had net practice on 5 and 12 June, and on 19 and 26 June we played an eleven-a-side tournament.

On 12 June, it was drizzling but the players were keen and did not give up. Kobe Gaidai sensei Yamada and ex-CA Paul Abraham finally succeeded in their persuading, and the first ball was hit at 2.40 p.m. but neither the rain nor we gave up and about seven of us played until 5 p.m.

The result was wonderful! Our Astroturf was completely soaked in rain, rainwater seeped in and a few drops were twinkling on the green bed and thick mud, on the rubber side. It was King Kong heavy and required eight tough guys to roll it out of the centre to a corner of the Isogami Ground and it took three sunny days to dry it out to normal so that three persons could roll it below the Billiard table!

On 19 June, we played a tournament. There were lots of Indian players but very few KR & AC members. There were several Gaidai members but they were short of a full team of eleven. Things were worked out to have two approximately equal strength teams but everything went out of control as a few players were excited, overconfident, overjoyed, but were just waiting to get padded, take a bat, snatch a ball, toss a coin. Anyway, they were geared up to hit, catch or run. Some of them had arrived quite early, before 2 p.m., and had already crowned themselves as captains and decided that it would be a no-captain or all captains team! Probably these cricket lovers were once team captains on their own schooldays therefore extremely overconfident, but this smart team lost to Kobe Gaidai, captained by Yamada sensei! 82 runs all out against 49 runs all out.

About 100 Japanese beauties (Kawaii neh!) from Shoin Women's University, turned up as spectators. We hope to have gallery seating soon! We had two lovely Japanese girls, playing, one in each team. They were good runners, no ball throwers but courageous enough to stand hard cricket balls. They made a few runs but were out in a few minutes. Dick Bell is backing out of forming his Scottish team. Hello KR & AC Ladies! What about forming a team? We will teach cricket, throw soft balls or speedy tennis balls. In India, the Indian Ladies play in Test Matches to raise funds for unexpected National calamities.

We are planning to organise everything properly so give us your support. If you have played cricket before or you want to learn the game, please turn up at the KR & AC on Sunday. We start at 2 p.m.

Reg-san, Sayonara. If we happen to play at Lord's, please join the KR & AC side. You did revive CRICKET just for that, didn't you?

*Kobe Regatta and Athletic Club Magazine*, July 1983

The trail is getting cold and our pavilions are becoming igloo shaped. But still the game goes on. Here are five frosty reports from Arctic and Antarctic regions, concluding at the South Pole itself.

# Whale of a Game

The Greenland instance is a recent event. An account of it was given by Mr S. E. Worm, headmaster of the senior school at the Sorø Skademi in Denmark, on the occasion of the official dinner given in conjunction with the notable Danish centenary cricket match played at Sorø. Mr Worm was in the company of some British geologists off the east coast of Greenland some years ago, when circumstances necessitated that their ship drop anchor awhile in the vicinity of Mestersvig. They decided to go ashore here, and an ingenious Scot among the party spied the remains of a stranded whale nearby on the beach. From this the party took some pieces of the ribs for stumps and two lengths of jaw-bone for bats, and with the aid of an empty instant-coffee tin one of the world's northernmost games of cricket was under way.

# Cricket in the South Atlantic

During my visit I had time to ask questions about cricket on both the Falklands and Ascension. As far as the Falklands is concerned ... cricket is not much played there. The only pitch is the paddock in the grounds of Government House in Port Stanley, where there are at present two sets of goal posts. The only attempt made to play cricket there since the war was ended by a snowstorm. However, interest is not dead, and many of us from the General downwards (David Thorne, a very keen and competent club and service cricketer) awaited with baited breath the World Service sports news with the scores of the fourth and fifth Tests in Australia. The Royal Navy Flag Officer who took over from Admiral Sir Sandy Woodward at the end of the war (Rear Admiral Ruffell) gave a trophy for an annual inter-service cricket competition – a broken wicket in wood. From what I saw there is enough flat ground at Ajax and Fitzroy Settlements to produce some sort of ground upon which cricket could be played – though I wouldn't answer for the state of the pitch – very low and slow because of the peaty soil. The only beach I saw which might have been fit for beach cricket was mined. There has been a game of cricket on Ascension between the Services and Cable & Wireless. The pitch there is matting on concrete, and a composition ball was used in order to reduce the pace and height of bounce. The outfield is made of volcanic ash – there is no grass – which does not encourage clean ground fielding.

'A SOLDIER'S REPORT' (written in January 1983), *Wisden*, 1984

# The Far South

As cricketers begin another English season, and curse the keen winds of early spring and the bulk of their several layers of sweaters, they might reflect on a historic game played last January – and think themselves fortunate.

Until then [serious] cricket matches had been played on every continent, save one. On 11 January that omission was remedied when an organised game of cricket between two full teams was played in Antarctica – the Gondwanaland Occasionals (captained by Chris Beeby of New Zealand) beating the Beardmore Casuals (captained by the present writer) by 27 runs.

The two teams were drawn from the participants – primarily scientists, diplomats, lawyers and environmentalists – in a workshop being held at the Beardmore South Camp in Antarctica under the auspices of the US National Academy of Science. We were a very international group, and on the two teams there were players of thirteen different nationalities, with three of the major cricketing countries contributing nearly half (Australia, New Zealand and the UK).

What makes this almost certainly the first full game in Antarctica is the sheer unlikelihood of a couple of dozen cricket-willing people having previously been together in one place on that frozen continent. Nor was it a game played on the outer edges of Antarctica, on its sometimes snow- and ice-free margins. This game was played on a glacier, at Beardmore South Camp which, at 84° South latitude, is only some four hundred miles from the South Pole. Both Shackleton and Scott had used the Beardmore Glacier, just a few miles away, as their route through the Transantarctic Mountains on their way to the Pole.

At an altitude of just over 6,000 feet and a temperature of about −14°C, and with the Polar ice cap for a playing field, the game had its unusual features.

Finding a suitable playing area presented some initial problems, but we eventually found ourselves an acceptable outfield of some nine inches of softly frozen snow lying on top of several hundred yards of glacier ice. This, however, would not have been good enough for the pitch itself. We needed a heavy roller, and found one in the form of a ski-equipped C-130 Hercules transport aircraft – perhaps, at about 50 tons, the heaviest heavy roller ever used. Along the lines of its several taxi-runs we had a level and tolerably firm square some ten yards wide and about a mile long.

The Beardmore Casuals, having lost the toss, batted first, and were given a good start by Roger Wilson of Greenpeace International, who made an aggressive 22 before climatic imperatives forced him (like many others during the game) to 'retire frozen' at the end of his allotted twelve balls. An elegant innings of 15 by Dick Woolcott (Australia) who looked altogether too much like a real cricketer, helped bring the innings to a comfortable 51 for five. But then two wickets by Geoffrey Larminie (UK), followed quickly by an acrobatic catch by Mitchell Wener (USA), began a collapse. Despite a daring late innings of 11 by John Gulland (UK), the Casuals' total reached no more than 102.

When the 'tea' interval was taken between innings at about 9.30 p.m., we were all much relieved (and some perhaps a little surprised) that the match was proving playable. If the Casuals were pleased to have at least made a three-figure score, the Gondwanaland Occasionals were glad to have no larger target to aim at. More seriously, however, such modest satisfaction with their efforts as both teams professed was eclipsed by the discovery that the beer at the side of the field had frozen.

This may have had something to do with the sedate start to the Occasionals' innings which, despite a resolute innings of 10 by Rolf Andersen (Norway), soon stood at 24 for three. The pitch was at last beginning to show increasing signs of wear, to say nothing of freezing. But Tucker Scully (USA), with a vivid, left-handed 16 (and, baseball style, a dropped bat each time he went for a run), and Zain Azraai (Malaysia), with a cheerful 12, restored the Occasionals' fortunes. A robust innings of 17 by Chris Beeby, who had clearly played cricket before, and a delicate innings of 11 by Lee Kimball (USA), who equally clearly had not but whose baseball experience was put to good effect, gave the innings a solid middle, leaving Trevor Hatherton (New Zealand) to put the issue beyond doubt with a forceful and stylish 24. The rest of the innings, which finally reached 129, was distinguished only by an eccentric but mercifully short innings by the President of Texas University (Bob Rutford), which occasioned scenes of excitability which the umpire could only restrain by adopting his most severe expression.

This unique match ended about an hour before midnight, with the sun still shining brightly in a clear blue sky. After post-match refreshments under the midnight sun, will the pavilion bar ever seem the same again?

A. D. WATTS, *The Cricketer*, June 1985

# A Polar Six

The record for cricket in unusual venues must go to the South Pole, where John Reid, the former New Zealand captain, struck a six into the snow and the ball – the only one they had – vanished. That venue may, in fact, rank as the strangest of them all. The wicket was the Pole itself, which at the time (1969) was represented by a striped barber's-type pole with a silvered reflecting glass ball on top. Another unique feature was that every shot played by the batsmen, no matter how they hit it, travelled north.

C. MARTIN-JENKINS, *The Cricketer Book of Bizarre Cricketing Records*

**In the company of our contributors we have eavesdropped on not a few games of cricket in many varied climes. Some-times, to be honest, our reports have not been free of irreverent humour. So, in conclusion, it seems only fair to turn the tables on ourselves. Here is the Sports Correspondent of the *Wall Street Journal* trying, with not the best of grace, to come to terms with the game as it is played in England.**

# As Others See Us

I first visited England a dozen years ago, and one of my main memories of the trip was picking up a British newspaper, reading a long story on the sports page, and not understanding a word of it. Even the identity of the sport was obscure.

I later learned that the game was cricket, which has a vocabulary all its own. This is mostly because British sportswriters have had much longer to hone their clichés than we Yanks. Reading about cricket now is what reading about baseball will be like in a hundred or so years.

Here's a brief sample of what I mean, from a recent *Times*: 'Gilbert had Gladwin held at long leg from a hook; Pritchard was caught behind off a lifting ball; and Lilly was leg before to one that kept low. In the first over bowled by Matthews, Gooch played a forcing stroke off his legs and was well caught, low down at short midwicket by Hilditch.'

The experience left me with two resolves: first, never to write a sports story without mentioning the sport, and, second, to see a cricket match. Anything that obscure must be interesting.

Summer is cricket season in England, so witnessing a match during my present trip was high on my agenda. Just where cricket ranks in the hearts of Englishmen was brought home to me on my first evening here, when I attended a function linked to the Wimbledon tennis tournament. I was introduced to a British tennis promoter, and was having a hard time making chitchat with him about the sport that provided his livelihood, until I told him I hoped to catch some cricket.

'Ah – there's the sport! The ultimate civilised game!' he exclaimed. 'In football [soccer to Americans] the players generally behave well but the fans carry on. In tennis, the fans behave but the players fuss. But in cricket, everyone is gentlemanly.'

But cricket's typical Britishness goes beyond an upper-class emphasis on manners. Cricket was invented here. And, like most things British, cricket matches take awhile. Countries play for five days, and county matches – the staple of English cricket – last for three. Recently, one-day cricket has taken hold, but rarely for important events. 'Can't develop any decent strategy in just a day,' I was told.

Furthermore, as often as not, matches end in draws. We Americans find stand-offs intolerable and invent tie-breakers and shoot-outs to eliminate them. The British merely shrug, noting that life often is inconclusive.

Cricket is played on a large lawn that's more or less round. Most of the action takes place on the 'pitch', a rectangle 66 feet long in the centre of the field. At each end of the pitch is a wicket, three 28-inch-high sticks with a bridge, or 'bail', across the top. There are eleven players to a side. A team bats until ten outs, or wickets, have been recorded against it. Then the other team bats. One turn at bat for both teams equals an inning, as in baseball. Two innings (not mine, thank goodness) make a game. If the trailing team can't complete its innings, the match is a draw.

The main actors are the pitchers, called 'bowlers', and the batsmen. Batsmen take the field two at a time, one guarding each wicket. Most wear protective leg and face guards.

Batsmen wielding paddle-shaped bats attempt to score runs by hitting the ball between or over the fielders in any direction (there are no foul balls) and crossing to the opposite wicket without being caught. Each cross is worth a run. If their hit clears the boundary of the field on the ground, their team gets four runs. If they clear it on the fly, it's worth six. That's exciting, but it rarely happens.

The bowler takes a running start and tries to retire the batter by hurling the ball past him on a bounce, knocking the bail off the wicket behind him. A batter also is out if his hit is caught on the fly, if a fielder knocks off a bail while he's running, or if the umpire rules that he blocked a pitch with his body that would otherwise have hit a wicket. The game is a lot more complicated, but that's the general idea.

A batter's turn lasts as long as he protects his wicket. He won't run unless he's reasonably sure he can score. That's what makes games so long. Most matches start at 11 a.m. and run until 6.30 p.m. or later, with breaks for lunch and tea, of course.

The contestants of the county match I witnessed were Middlesex and Nottinghamshire. Barlow, Middlesex's lead-off man, slapped the ball to and fro and was approaching an individual 100 runs before lunch, a signal achievement. Alas, at 97 his tipped shot was caught by the wicketkeeper, cricket's version of a baseball catcher, and he was out. Run production slackened after that, although my press-box colleagues were divided on whether good bowling or poor batsmanship was the primary cause. One fellow stayed put for twenty or so hits before risking a dash for the opposite wicket and a run. The crowd cheered derisively. His effort was too slow even for cricket.

About the best thing that happened in the afternoon is that I learned a cricket joke. To get it, you need to know that a 'maiden' in cricket is when a bowler completes his turn of six pitches, or 'over', without surrendering a run.

Joke: 'Cricket is the only place where a fellow can bowl over a maiden and remain a gentleman.' Ho ho ho.

Middlesex tallied 246 runs before going out at 5.35 p.m. Notts posted 66 in only one wicket by quitting time, and its prospects for the match looked good. It would have to proceed without me, however. If nothing else, cricket made me appreciate the hours for baseball writing.

FREDERICK C. KLEIN, *Wall Street Journal*, 1985